Gould, Allan, 1944-
Canned lit : (parodies regained, then frozen and thawed) / Allan Gould ; illustrated by Graham Pilsworth. -- Toronto : Stoddart, 1990.
227 p. : ill.

04678567 ISBN:0773754334 (pbk.)

1. Authors, Canadian (English) - Anecdotes. 2. Authors, Canadian (English) - Humor. 3. Canadian literature (English) - History and criticism - Humor. 4. Canadian wit and humor (English) I. Pilsworth, Graham, 1944- II.
(SEE NEXT CARD)

Canned Lit

ALLAN GOULD

Canned Lit

(PARODIES REGAINED, THEN FROZEN and THAWED)

Illustrated by
GRAHAM PILSWORTH

First published in 1990 by
Stoddart Publishing Co. Limited
34 Lesmill Road
Toronto, Canada
M3B 2T6

CANADIAN CATALOGUING IN PUBLICATION DATA

Gould, Allan, 1944-
Canned lit

ISBN 0-7737-2417-6

1. Authors, Canadian (English) - Anecdotes.*
2. Authors, Canadian (English) - Humor.*
3. Canadian literature (English) - History and criticism - Humor.* 4. Canadian wit and humor (English).* I. Title.

PS8081.G68 1990 C818'.5402 C90-094401-3
PR9186.2.G68 1990

Typesetting: Tony Gordon Ltd.

Printed in Canada

To my wife, Merle, who teaches Canadian Literature so brilliantly, and our children, Judah and Elisheva, who are just now beginning to love Can Lit

Preface

C*anned Lit* needs no introduction, so we'll call this a preface and let it go at that. The book you just dropped awkwardly on the floor, and therefore have to buy, is a collection of profiles of the Major Canadian Authors, as well as (whenever applicable, possible or wise) an attempt to parody some of their writings and much of their style.

What's interesting, of course, is that there are *enough* Great Canadian Poets, Playwrights, Novelists and Short story Writers *worth* profiling and parodying. Two decades ago, this book would have given paper cuts. Half a century ago, it would have been a pamphlet. (And a helluva lot cheaper, too. Back then, one could buy a house in Toronto's Rosedale or Vancouver's British Properties for about $20,000, so everything is relative.)

The origin of this book can be traced back to this writer's youth, when I fell in love with the books of the great humorist Richard Armour. His *Classics Reclassified*, *English Lit Relit*, *American Lit Relit* and *Twisted Tales from Shakespeare* could be uneven (and what author is not?), but when they were on the mark, they were hysterical. (I still laugh at his suggestion that Hester Prynne wears a scarlet letter A "because she's dating an Amherst boy.") Several years ago, when down in Los Angeles to do some profiles for *Chatelaine*, I spent an entire afternoon with that kind and gifted man, then eighty years of age, and was able to tell him of my lifelong love for his work. When he passed away in 1989, I felt that I had lost a personal hero.

But enough of the maudlin stuff. This is supposed to be hard-hitting parody and satire — as well as some nifty history — on more than 100 Canadian authors and their writings, saving readers big bucks on Coles Notes. As a longtime student (and occasional sufferer) of Can Lit, I believe that I know it, and care for it sufficiently, to personhandle it as I have done here. Let the final words be from that famous non-Canadian Ernest Hemingway, who *did* work for the *Toronto Star* for a while (see **Callaghan, Morley**), hating every minute of it. He once told his biographer, A. E. Hotchner, "The parody is the last refuge of the frustrated writer. . . . The greater the work of literature, the easier the parody. The step up from writing parodies is writing on the wall above the urinal."

How can I argue with the man our own Morley Callaghan once knocked on his rear — and in Paris yet? And so, here are my thanks to those many Canadian writers who wrote well enough to make my job easy.

Allan Gould

Canned Lit

Milton Acorn

(1923 –   )

Known as the "People's Poet" (even if the People never seem to want to buy books of poetry), Milton Acorn was born in Charlottetown, P.E.I. After living in Montreal, Toronto and Vancouver (where he helped found the successful "underground" newspaper *Georgia Straight*, one of the few unbent things in B.C.), he became committed to Marxism, long before Mikhael Gorbachev and Eastern Europe turned against it. Among his most important collections of poems are *Jackpine Sonnets* and the slightly earlier *I've Tasted My Blood: Poems 1956 to 1968*, which had the distinct honour of not receiving a Governor General's Award. Indeed, since Acorn was a carpenter before he turned full time to poetry, it is understandable why he tasted his blood so much. Many Canadian carpenters have similar trouble with their tools.

Margaret Atwood

(1939 –   )

Probably Canada's best-known novelist, as well as Canada's less-well-known poet and least-well-known short story writer, Margaret Atwood was born in Ottawa, but had the good fortune to spend much of her youth with her entomologist father in a log cabin in northern Quebec. There she experienced firsthand the difficulty of survival and the terror of the bush. Her father's specialty was insects, which in his elder daughter's hands would evolve into her own expertise: men who bug women.

Her first collection of poems, *The Circle Game*, won a Governor General's medal in 1966. The award not only doubled the book's sales (to 103 copies), but gave Atwood enough money to buy a pair of contact lenses. This inspired one of her most famous poems:

> You fit into me
> like a harpoon
> in an eye
> a harpoon
> an open eye
> ow
> eh?

Poetry continued to flow from Atwood's old typewriter like bad poems from **Irving Layton**'s: *The Animals in That Country* in 1968 (it was the men who were usually the animals); *The Journals of Susanna Moodie* in 1970 (a lot better than the original, if you ask me); *Power Politics* in 1973 (with the men holding all the power, unfortunately); *You Are Happy* in 1974 (she would have been happier if it hadn't been for all those damned men); *Two-headed Poems* in 1978 (and two female heads are better than one . . .); *True Stories* in 1981 (which were true, of course, because a woman told them); and a number of others, all of them fighting against evil and man unkind.

There were short story collections, as well (*Dancing Girls* and *Bluebeard's Castle*, which contained few stories that would remind one of **Alice Munro**, except to make one long for Alice Munro), and even a seminal (if you'll pardon the male image; it might be more correct to say ovumular) book of criticism, *Survival: A Thematic Guide to Canadian Literature.* In it Atwood proved beyond a shadow of a doubt that Canadians are by nature victims, pathologically attracted to failure. This, of course, is proven not only in this country's writings, but in such Canada-wide examples as Montreal's backing of the Expos, Toronto's backing of the Maple Leafs, and all backers of the federal Liberal party west of Manitoba.

But it is with her growing number of novels that Margaret Atwood has gained a name for herself, as well as the one she was born with and refuses to change for any man, even Graeme Gibson: *The Edible Woman* (which many male critics found inedible); *Lady Oracle* (which led other male critics to insist "That was no lady; she is my strife"); *Surfacing* (which yet other male critics claimed was "not deep"); *Life Before Man* (which was the only time in history when life was worth living, Atwood implies); *Bodily Harm* (which is all that most women can expect from men); *The Handmaid's Tale* ("which is only *her* side of the story," argued some male critics); and *Cat's Eye* (which was the cat's pajamas to most female critics, who are finally managing to get published, and it's about time, too).

Since Ms. Atwood has become such a major force in Canadian publishing — and, more important, her books are read and even admired in the United States, England,

Australia and Europe, so they must be pretty good — I shall attempt to share some of the plots of her most famous novels with you. Of course, I'm only a man, so what the hell could *I* know?

THE PLOT OF *SURFACING* (1972)

IN THIS STORY of a young woman's search for her lost father in the Canadian wilderness, the reader wonders why any woman would want to waste her time searching for some lousy man. The unnamed narrator is an artist who takes three friends into the woods to try to find Daddy, who has gone to live alone on a small lake near the Ontario/Quebec border, where even the fish are forced to be bilingual. The four young people are Joe, the boyfriend of our heroine, who is a lousy potter, because that's just the way these men are; Anna, her best friend (but we learn many years later in *Cat's Eye* just how trustworthy best friends can be); and David, Anna's husband, and therefore not Anna's best friend at all.

This charming Gang of Four spends a week up at the island, maiming fish, picking berries and picking on one another. (You know what these men are like.) The young narrator finds weird and primitive drawings, as weird and primitive as men are, and she eventually must dive off a cliff in order to heal her tortured soul and accept her father's death. Of course, if fathers would only grow up already, their daughters wouldn't all be so tortured. The father's body is eventually dragged up, while the daughter must cleanse herself in the lake to be reborn, which sure sounds like a male-oriented-and-run religion we've read about. But there is still happiness to be found here, if only because the father did not live long enough to suffer through the fiasco of a Canadian movie based on the book, which was so awful that even the Canadian pay-TV movie channels won't play it, and they need all the Canadian content they can get.

FROM *LIFE BEFORE MAN* (1979)

CHRIS, THE FORMER LOVER of Elizabeth Schoenhof, the protagonist, kills himself just before the novel begins, which is not surprising, because some men will do anything to avoid their responsibilities to women. Chris had worked in the same natural history museum where Elizabeth and Lesje still work; the latter is about to become Elizabeth's husband Nate's new lover, which only goes to show the importance of safe sex. And if this isn't enough, Nate, Elizabeth's husband, has just finished up a love affair with Martha, a secretary in his law firm, which shouldn't shock any wife who has the misfortune of being married to a lawyer. (And the Canadian Civil Liberties Union questions the importance of mandatory AIDS testing?)

Nate now latches on to Lesje, primarily because only he can pronounce her name, and gets her to leave William, with whom Lesje was living before and an unimportant character, since he's only a man. By the end of the novel, Elizabeth has asked for a divorce from Nate, who shouldn't mind too much because he's got lots of girls, anyway, and Lesje has stopped taking birth control pills, which should come as a nice seven pound, four ounce surprise to the dirty cheater Nate when he finally realizes what she's done. Why women even stay with men, other than to get pregnant, is the key question here, since it is clear that life before man was probably a lot more pleasant when there may have been only self-impregnating women, who didn't have to spend all their time sleeping with the enemy.

FROM *THE HANDMAID'S TALE*
(1986)

IT'S ROUGH TIMES, AS USUAL, for women. Fanatical Protestant fundamentalists have taken over the United States and established the Republic of Gilead, where, much as in the world of the late 1980s, women have no rights: they can't hold jobs; they are not allowed to have money or property; and they must stay out of sight. Thanks to the pollution of the world — caused by men, natch — there has been a growing sterility, so handmaids are used to bear children for important men — just like today! These uteruses on two legs are given the names of the men who use them: for instance, Ofmordecai, Offarley, Ofpierre — you know.

Our heroine is Offred (since no reader would ever believe a name like Offarley), who must present herself regularly to the commander for sex — one reason this book will never make the Grade Nine Required Reading List in Saskatchewan. Much of the book is taken up with Offred thinking of the good old days, when she had a daughter and when sex was actually fun, even though it was still with men. Things get really sexy when we read how the commander loves to play board and card games with Offred, when all he should really be doing is making nonerotic love to her, just as in most other Canadian novels. Meanwhile, the commander's wife, Serena Joy, is concerned that Offred has not become pregnant, so she fixes her up with the commander's chauffeur, Nick, who actually makes love for fun (!), an idea that had yet to catch on in Canada when the novel was written in the mid-1980s. Offred escapes to

Canada, which as the ten million Canadians in Florida at this very moment will be pleased to verify, is *no* place to escape to, even to get away from the Republic of Gilead. The book ends with a hilarious epilogue in which historians, meeting more than a century after the book takes place, discuss the book in literary terms, ignoring the brutal mistreatment of women during Offred's time. Just like historians and literary critics in the 1990s.

ARCHIBALD BELANEY

(1888 – 1938)

ALTHOUGH he was an Englishman who passed himself off as Grey Owl, a hugely popular writer and speaker between World War I and World War II, when he died Belaney was believed to be an Ojibwa Indian. He wrote four books, lectured across the United States and Britain and even spoke before the royal family at Buckingham Palace. The *Times* of London called him a "Canadian Thoreau," when he wasn't even a thorough Canadian, much less thoroughly Indian. One can only imagine what would happen if **W. P. Kinsella** and **Rudy Wiebe** were actually discovered to be Indians. Would they still be considered racist for writing about native people?

CONSTANCE BERESFORD-HOWE

(1922 –)

MONTREAL-BORN and McGill-educated, Beresford-Howe is the most-important hyphen-filled Canadian-writer to-day. While she has well-crafted more than a half-dozen novels about young-women, Beresford-Howe's greatest-success has been *The Book of Eve*, which tells about a middle-class woman who decides-to-leave her quite-sickly, pain-in-the-ass husband so she can be free-at-last. It's damned-good.

PIERRE BERTON

(1920 –   )

BORN in Whitehorse, Yukon, a fact he won't let any of his fellow Canadians ever forget, Pierre Francis de Marigny Berton embarked on his nonstop writing career at an early age, publishing his stick drawings and his mother's private scrawls while still in preschool (*Drawings and Grocery Lists*, McKlondike and Stewart, 1924). Soon after came an anthology of personal recollections (*My Summer Vacations*, General Publishing Braggart, 1929), followed quickly by memorabilia (*Notes I Passed in Class That Were Never Intercepted by Mrs. Dixon*, House of Klondike Press, Ltd., 1933).

After studying at the University of British Columbia, Berton became city editor of the Vancouver *News-Herald*, an experience he described at interminable length in the first of a prospective twenty-volume autobiography entitled *Great Pierre's Starting Out*, which he finally got around to publishing in 1987. Then it was off to win World War II, which, interestingly, managed to become famous as a war without him, something that can be said about few other wars Canadians have been involved in.

Back in Vancouver after the war, Berton was a feature writer for the *Sun* before joining *Maclean's* in 1947 and serving as its managing editor from 1952 to 1958. It was here that he quickly churned out (and we're choosing our words very carefully) *Hot off the Press at Maclean's* (1948);

From the Wastebaskets at Maclean's (1948, coauthored with the cleaning lady of the time, Mrs. Mavis Flanagan); and *The Ever-changing Menu at the Maclean-Hunter Commissary* (1953). The latter book eventually caught the interest of the publishers of Canada's largest, most wishy-washy newspaper, the *Toronto Star*, whose commissary had been dreadful until that time. He joined the staff of that so-called newspaper in 1958 as a columnist and associate editor, winning awards for writing the most columns and books ever in one year without using steroids.

By 1962, Berton had had enough of the *Star* (it took Hemingway far less time to wise up), and left to work briefly at *Maclean's* again. Then he moved into television, where he promptly replaced Mister Chichimus as Canada's favourite personality. The programs were ubiquitous, and all showed a little bit of what made the brilliant man tick: "The Pierre Berton Show," "The Show Starring Pierre Berton," "Berton!," "Berton's Country," "My Country 'Tis of Berton," "Attacking Berton," "Berton under Attack," "Berton's Debate," "Oh, Pierre!," "For Love of Berton," "All in the Berton," "The Six-Million-Dollar Berton," "Berton 5-0" (which ran only the year he turned that age), "Berton's Company," "My Three Bertons,"

"The Wonder Berton," "Golden Berton" and his longest-running success, "B*E*R*T*O*N." Understandably, the transcripts of every show were rushed into print, and even more quickly into remaindership.

During this same period, the extraordinary fellow also wrote and published *Just Add Berton and Stir* and *The Cool Crazy Committed World of Berton* (both in 1962), *The Comfortable Berton* (and by this time he surely was; 1965), *Smug Berton* (and can you blame him?; 1968) and *Fast Fast Fast Berton* (a title no Canadian could argue with; 1969).

In terms of his literary career, which means we can ignore all the above, Pierre Berton has managed to become one of the most widely read and admired popular historians in the world, writing such impressive tomes as *Klondike* (1958), in which he not only described the fascinating personalities of the men who moiled for gold, but even explained what the hell "moil for gold" meant; *The National Dream* and *The Last Spike* (1970 and 1971), a two-volume history of the Canadian Pacific Railway, which used to be a way of getting across the country (published in one volume as *The Impossible Railway* for the American market, but Coles Books was kind enough to bring several hundred thousand remaindered copies across the border to save Canadians lots of money and drive Berton nuts; *The Invasion of Canada* and *Flames Across the Border* (1980 and 1981), reminding us that the United States had once invaded Canada many years before its movies and television did; and countless other books that are too numerous to enumerate, and thus should have been too numerous to write, as well. Berton also has eight children, showing that his prolific nature has not been limited to newspapers, magazines, television shows and books.

By telling us more than we ever wanted to know about

ourselves, and by wiping out more than one-quarter of Canadian forests in order to print his hundreds of best-selling books, Pierre Berton has had a profound impact on this country's history, heritage, self-understanding, booksellers and, ultimately, trees.

FROM *ALL HIS BOOKS PUT TOGETHER*
(1926 – 1989)

IT WAS BITTER COLD in the Klondike, but the men could tell that it was cold, without even knowing it in Fahrenheit or centigrade. As their toes began to turn green and fall off, they would stare at one another and mumble, "Cold enough fur ya?" But the railway *would* be completed, no matter how many more delays took place. Cornelius Van Horne wasn't about to let those workmen stop his dream, in spite of any idiots in Ottawa who might come along more than a century later and drive a last spike into the railroad's heart.

Of course, if the church really *wanted* to stand for something, it would, though from the way it has been going, it will stand for anything. But the bullets kept flying, forcing the underarmed farmers to take cover behind their bales of hay; the "f——ing Yankees" (to quote directly from countless letters mailed at this time) weren't about to be stopped. It wasn't the Dionnes who were at fault, of course. It was the good doctor, and a Depression-era public longing for everything they could read about the five obnoxious little twits.

Then the world seemed to explode, as the longest and most ferocious artillery barrage in human history burst upon the surprised Germans, initiating the Battle of Vimy Ridge. Who knew then that this was a stupid, useless, blood war? Naturally, it wasn't Queen Victoria's fault. Albert, as always, had been breaking wind during the royal dinner, mortifying everyone within three blocks and gassing half the people in the room.

Hollywood had always had this idiotic way of looking at Canada, which is justifiable in retrospect, since there has rarely been a more idiotic country. The men shivered, the men froze, the men cursed, but they were determined to work their way into the bowels of the Arctic at last, knowing they were a lot safer there than the bowels of Victoria's consort. They knew in their heart of hearts that anything, yes, anything, was possible in the secret world of Og.

There are many good reasons why we act like Canadians, not the least of which is that we can never seem to get enough green cards to allow *all* of us to work in the States. And if there is anything more smug than a Protestant/capitalist member of the Liberal or Conservative party, I haven't yet met him. Sadly, their numbers are legion, and it's a damned shame that they weren't all wiped out at Vimy or scalped by Tecumseh in 1813. My countless children gathered around our boat, anxious to continue our glorious journey up, or maybe it was down, the dangerous river and hoped against hope to be immortalized in their beloved father's writing, while *not* having to be shot at by Americans or Germans, or not having to freeze their little buns off somewhere in the frozen northern wastes. The recipe for *Poulet à la canadienne* begins like all others from that special part of French Canada:

> Steal one chicken, then sneak into the garden of an Anglo and grab some vegetables. Then find some large pot and measure out three litres of water, which you bring quickly to moil. . . .

Earle Birney

(1904 –)

Born in Calgary in 1904, Earle Birney spent much of his youth on an isolated farm in northern Alberta, communing with nature but unfortunately not commuting to civilization. Finally his family moved to Banff, where foolish teachers encouraged his reading, never suspecting that the child might turn to writing someday.

After earning enough money to attend university by working at a number of manual jobs, preparing him for a life at a manual typewriter, Birney entered the University of British Columbia in 1922, hoping to study chemical engineering. Four years later, he graduated with first-class honours in English, prepared for nothing whatsoever and showing an obvious confusion in career goals. It is noteworthy that he edited the famous campus newspaper *Ubyssey*, which would soon see thousands of well-crafted and well-written articles by **Pierre Berton** and, much later, the facetious scribblings of Allan Fotheringham. Yet both those men have penned major Canadian best-sellers. There's a moral there somewhere.

Then it was off to California, Utah and New York, where he worked for the Trotskyites, an early rock group whose rocks were primarily in their heads. Indeed, Birney even went off to Norway in 1935 to interview the one-time Bolshevik leader, and got arrested in Germany "for not saluting a Nazi parade." This showed his genuine sense of morality. Still, Birney probably would have saluted a Communist parade during those years, something that would move most Canadians to wonder about his genuine sense of morality. (To be fair, when one looks at the VanDer-

Zalmish political leadership back home in Ottawa during those same years — R. B. Bennett and William Lyon Mackenzie King — one can understand any sane person in the 1930s longing to salute at a pit bull parade.)

Back in Canada, Birney completed his Ph.D. in English at the University of Toronto in 1936, in which he saluted Chaucer's parade. He also served as the literary editor of *Canadian Forum* magazine and began to publish poems. It was exceedingly late for most poets to start displaying their work, but somehow this country had been willing to wait. It had the Great Depression, World War II and, even worse, Bennett and Mackenzie King to contend with.

The next few decades were extremely fruitful ones for Birney. He began to teach English and, eventually, creative writing at the University of British Columbia; he edited *Canadian Poetry* magazine; he won a Governor General's Award for *Now Is Time*; he wrote a highly successful humorous novel about the Canadian Army called *Turvey*; he published *Near False Creek Mouth*; and, while criss-crossing the entire world, giving poetry readings, he continued to turn out poetry collections faster than the Soviet Union, the United States and, in its usual puppy-dog fashion, Canada, were throwing out Trotskyites.

Birney's most anthologized work is "David," a lengthy, nine-part poem about the poet and a friend climbing several Canadian mountains without the help of Sherpas or a Canada Council grant. The title character falls to his death, but not before he holds several extended conversations with the poet ("Bob"), many of them almost rhyming and all of them awkward. David doesn't have a chance, of course. This is Canada, where anywhere more than a fifteen-minute drive from Halifax, Montreal, Ottawa, Winnipeg, Calgary, Edmonton or Vancouver is dangerous bush. (In Toronto, even downtown is dangerous bush, and bush league, as well.) But the poet survives, and goes on to write and publish tens of thousands of other poems, making the readers of "David" question whether the right person survived.

bill bissett

(1939 –)

tHE drug-using, dirty-language-using, capital-letter-rejecting bard of vancouver has published nearly four dozen volumes of po'try, most of it mispeled, much of it nayeve, sum of it baynel but occasionally kinda fun, which is reel canadyan ov him, even tho heez into SEX, wich this countree haz tended to froun on, yu no?

NEIL BISSOONDATH

(1955 –)

IT sure doesn't hurt to have famous relatives.

MARIE-CLAIRE BLAIS

(1939 –)

BORN in Quebec City at a time when service was still available in English, Marie-Claire Blais left school while in her early teens to work in a shoe factory. It would be only a few years before she would give the boot to Canadian literature, as well as to her native province.

By the time she was twenty, Blais had published *La Belle Bête*, known to English readers as *Mad Shadows*, since insanity has always interested Anglos more than beauty. It was the beginning of a remarkable career of describing Canada as only its poets, and seventy-five percent of its citizens, knew it: nasty priests, vicious nuns, doomed children, crushed relationships and destructive parents, with evil and madness abounding — sort of like a gathering of the Alberta and British Columbia Social Credit parties.

Mad Shadows came out in 1959 — she was barely out of her teens when she wrote it! (If you can get your kids away from the Nintendo long enough, ask them why the hell *they* can't show such talent. On second thought, considering what the book is about, maybe it's better if the kids hang out at the mall.) The book is pure Canadiana: a train, a lake, an isolated city, a house in the country. As well as an envious daughter (Isabelle-Marie), a physically attractive but stupid son (Patrice), their dull mother (Louise) and a friend (Michael), who is sightless until he regains his sight and thus rejects Isabelle-Marie, we also encounter cruelty, envy, maiming, drowning and murder. Sort of like a federal Progressive Conservative Party leadership review.

In 1965 came *Une Saison dans la vie d'Emmanuel*, daringly translated as *A Season in the Life of Emmanuel* in the following year. It is a kindly, sweet tale to which any Québécois can relate: an illiterate farmer and his extremely tired wife live with their sixteen children and no maid in a home lacking love, hope or promise. Jean Le Maigre dies of tuberculosis; one daughter longs to go to a brothel, where she can find some respect; only the grandmother, Antoinette, has some hope, probably because she's too old to get pregnant every seven months. In a nutshell, the entire household is going to hell in a handbag that ain't Gucci — sort of like a federal Liberal Party convention.

Blais also wrote three semiautobiographical novels about a young woman growing up in Quebec, which are even happier. The first of them (*Les Manuscrits de Pauline Archange*) won a Governor General's Award for Viciousness to French Canadians, handed over to the gifted young writer just as soon as the governor general stopped blushing. Ms. Blais has written several other novels and works of poetry. When taken together, they make the strongest argument for ratifying the Meech Lake Accord, since they make clear that Quebec is, inarguably, a distinct society.

FRANCES BROOKE

(1724 – 1789)

MRS. Frances Brooke, known to her many admirers as "Mrs.," joined the high ranks of Canadian literature at an early stage in this country's history because she filled most of the important criteria: she was white, she was Protestant, she was British and she was publishing when no one else was. It's true she lacked the single most important thing needed to be a truly respected writer*, but she made up for it in a very special way: she actually lived in Canada and wrote in Canada during an era when people all over the civilized world were asking one another daily, "If you're that good, why aren't you in England?"

Indeed, Mrs. Brooke, born Frances Moore in Lincolnshire in 1724, was the daughter of a minister, a patrilineal descent almost as important at this time as being born in England. And she actually was born in England. So maybe she *was* "that good," after all.

* a penis

While little is known of her early life, since *Private Eye* had not yet started publication, we do know that by the mid-1750s she was already in London, editing a weekly periodical.

Then, in 1756, having been so impressed with her father's work, she married a reverend, John Brooke. Yet, unlike so many women over the two-centuries-plus that have followed, she actually continued to put pen to paper, to the horror of publishers and readers across the Mother Country. (Do note that Mrs. Brooke was not yet Canadian, since she hadn't visited this country by this time.)

The very year Frances Moore was submerged into Frances Brooke, she published a volume of poems, fortunately lost, and translated a French romance in 1760, nearly leading to another war between the two longtime enemies.

Then, in 1763, Mrs. Brooke heard the words that had struck terror in the hearts of many hundreds of young women during that time. (No, they were *not* "The Canada Council has declined your application for a grant" — she could only have seen those words some two hundred years later.) The horrifying words came from her husband: "Darling, I've been appointed chaplain of the British garrison at Quebec."

Mrs. Brooke's response has echoed throughout history, to the point where it is heard daily across much of the Prairies and the Canadian West to this very day: *"Where's Quebec?"*

Knowing that any semblance of fun and civilization were over for her for the foreseeable future, the blossoming writer refused to join her husband for a while so she could complete her first novel, *The History of Lady Julia Mandeville*, and see it to press. (To get it to readers was quite another matter.)

By the end of 1763, however, she was forced to join her

husband in Quebec. It was a long and arduous journey, since Via Rail wasn't working then, either.

Mrs. Brooke found Quebec harsh, brutal and unforgiving, much as did the federal Tories until 1984 and the NDP to this day. In fact, by November of 1764, just one year after she had arrived on Canadian shores, she returned to England for a while, relieved to see English-language signs on both the outside as well as the inside of all buildings. Or to see actual buildings, for that matter.

By 1768, the Brookes had had enough. It was too painful for Frances Brooke to walk into a Quebec bookstore and find only a single shelf labelled "Canadian Literature," a shelf that was always empty, to boot. The good man and his wife sold their belongings and headed back to England, even though the Reverend Brooke continued to draw his army pay as chaplain of the Quebec garrison for another twenty years without working there again. (This tradition has been preserved all over Newfoundland, especially since 1949.)

Tragically for students of Canadian literature, Mrs. Brooke did put out a book in 1769, called *The History of Emily Montague*. It was published back in England, of course, since McClelland and Stewart was barely a gleam in Canada's eye during her time.

What made this book so very important was not that it was written in Canada — we cannot even be sure about that — but that it was *about* Canada, a country most Canadian-born authors wouldn't use as a background well into the twentieth century.

Emily Montague came out in four volumes, a fact that troubled many readers, until they realized it could have been published in a half-dozen volumes or more. It was reprinted in 1777 and 1784, then translated into French in an ugly attempt to get back at Mrs. Brooke for having translated that French romance into English some years earlier.

Frances Brooke continued to publish various other works of fiction in England for several more years, but luckily they were not about Canada, so no one is obliged to read them today, even in the most stringent Canadian literature course.

Finally Mrs. Brooke stopped writing in January 1789, since that was when she died. Her husband had died three days earlier, so it is understandable that she would die so soon after. Recall that she had always followed the reverend, even to Quebec.

FROM *THE HISTORY OF EMILY MONTAGUE*

LETTER XLIVQ

To Miss Johnson, Claridge Street [London]

Hull, January 1

It is hard even to breathe, darling; the cold is so horrible you'd think we were posted in Winnipeg. It must be thirty below, Fahrenheit, and only the Good Lord knows what that could be in centigrade. It is so cold, my dear friend, that an exhibitionist went up to me yesterday, outside the fort, and described himself. I have lots of things to do at Quebec; alas, the stove is terribly heavy to carry with me when I go there. And this is June yet. (Joke.)

We have had some nine days of dreadful weather. So cold, in truth, that many of the horses can't be jump-started in the morning, even if you had plugged them in the previous night. The natives complain bitterly about the cold; but, fortunately, their words of protest will not thaw out until next August, when we'll have to listen to them once more, alas. Everyone bitches about the cold, but they've never spent a February in a London house without central heating, so what do *they* know??

Even the wine freezes, and that's while it sits on the stove yet. Still, it's nice not to have to chill the champagne when you want it cold. But if you want to drink something at room temperature, it's h-ll to accomplish.

I must be off to Quebec tomorrow, or maybe I'll have company here, I'm not sure. It is so necessary to have people around at all times, so we can rub against one another a bit.

I used to wonder why there is no culture in this land, but who can doubt the reason now? The strings on the violin bow would freeze; the paint on the easel would turn to ice; the tongue in the mouth of the singer would stick to her roof; the movement of the actor would be impossible, unless the theatre set were taken down and burned to create some warmth.

No, greatness in the arts can never amount to much in this godforsaken land, unless some kind of grants agency were set up to give free stoves to potential writers and artists. Now there's a fine idea.

A group of men came to our community yesterday, notwithstanding the bitter cold. It is a Canadian custom to visit the ladies on New Year's Day and to kiss them. It supposedly helps to keep one warm; with an English kiss, just maybe.

The men all look like bears, since they are wrapped in fur from head to toe. All you see are their noses, and the long icicles that hang down from each. Some of the icicles are pretty erotic, but that's about it. One wonders how all those beavers are managing without their fur; they must be freezing half to death.

The ladies are equally covered up, although more in cloaks than fur. And to think that future generations will wonder how we in the eighteenth century practiced birth control! The weather does it for us.

My suitor, Captain Fitzgerald, is hot stuff compared to this weather. But, then, a Greek statue would be hot stuff compared to this weather. Even a clothed one.

I have been drinking liqueur to keep warm, and it helps. Actually, I've been drinking Scotch to keep warm. Come to think of it, I've been drinking whiskey to keep warm. Then again, I've been. . . Dearest friend, I do believe that I'm drunk. I'll write again when my ink thaws.

Yours,
Arabella F.

LETTER LXMFT

To Miss Johnson, Claridge Street [London]

Hell, February 31

It is warmer now. I'm wearing only seven petticoats today, instead of the usual nineteen. The men are dressing more like sheep instead of bears, which is a distinct turn-on, especially if you are into sheep, or vice versa.

It is actually a wonderful thing to be a woman here in Canada. There are about twenty-three men to every woman, and that doesn't even count the aboriginals, who don't count, anyway. Meanwhile, the liqueur is sustaining me. As is the Scotch. As is the whiskey. As is . . .

Darling, I'll write again when I'm sober.

Yours in forty proof,
Arabella F.

LETTER XXBOOZE

To Miss Johnson, Claridge Street [London]

Palm Springs, May 10

Good news. I have been drying out in this detox centre run by Martha Washington, the wife of a nice general from south of the border. She has done wonders with people who have "drinking problems," such as myself. It appears that the vast majority who have been in this programme are from Canada, which could get back to the cold I have described in my previous letters.

Meanwhile, it is easy to understand why there are no arts in this dreadful British protectorate, or whatever they call this country. It is so dreadfully hot here! How hot is it, you ask? It's so hot, I saw a snake shed five layers of skin, then . . .

Yours till Niagara Falls,
Arabella F.

ERNEST BUCKLER

(1908 – 1984)

KNOWN as the man who singlehandedly put Entremont, Nova Scotia, on the map, to the great relief of the Canadian Automobile Association, Ernest Buckler was born in Dalhousie West, a tiny Maritime village. He was educated in a local one-room schoolhouse, then at the two-bit Dalhousie University and the three-ring University of Toronto, where he obtained an M.A. in philosophy. Though he was offered a fellowship toward a Ph.D., ill health sent him back to the family farm. (This is most unusual. Normally it is the ill health of farms that sends its inhabitants to the big cities.) For five years in the early 1930s, Buckler laboured in the actuarial department of a Toronto insurance company, putting his philosophy background to work, before singing "Farewell to Old Hog Town" and returning to a farm of his own near Bridgetown, a similar world-class city in Nova Scotia.

During the 1940s and 1950s, a steady stream of wheat, milk and short stories poured out of Buckler's farm, the latter appearing in *Maclean's*, *Saturday Night*, *Coronet* and *Esquire*. The former landed on kitchen tables across the Maritimes.

Until his death in the mid-1980s, Buckler wrote numerous short stories, essays and a few novels, including *The Cruelest Month* (1963), *Ox Bells and Fireflies* (1968), *Window on the Sea* (1973) and *Whirligig* (1977). But his most important and greatest achievement was his first novel, *The Mountain and the Valley* (1952), a study of the unfulfilled writer in this country, something Buckler spent the next three decades proving.

The novel is highly symbolic — the family is called Canaan (when everyone knows that the Atlantic provinces are really Philistinic); the hero is named David; his brother is called Christopher; his parents are called Martha and Joseph — and so were the book's sales. Few North Americans, except the handful studying Canadian literature, found a book about the inner feelings of an oversensitive child in a small Annapolis Valley village to be of pressing interest.

But they were missing something. What could be of greater interest than a thirty-year-old kid staring endlessly at a valley and a mountain and an aged grannie who is forever hooking together rugs from the detritus of the family and parents who are inarticulate?

Oh, lots of things.

Anyway, the book has some hot sex, thank heavens. Young David, feeling sorry for a girlfriend, Effie, whose father drowned (that's probably symbolic, as well; in great Canadian literature, people are always drowning when they're not freezing to death), kisses her on the stage during a school Christmas play. This is hot stuff for Maritimers, who don't believe in kissing in a play unless the performers have been married for several years, and so they banish young David. Rather than move to New England, as the majority of eastern Canadians are forced to do, he chooses to become a superior student and sit around watching everyone else work, much like a member of the Civil Service in Ottawa.

Passion doesn't work out too well for young David, who realizes that in the Canada of the 1920s, safe sex just doesn't exist. When David first does "it" (a euphemism; don't panic) with Effie, he chooses *not* to do "it" onstage during another Christmas play, yet is still discovered during the act by some other children. (Coitus interruptus was always acceptable to the Catholic Church, helping to keep this novel off the Index.) Then, when the young couple tries "it" again, the girl has a cold and soon dies from leukemia, teaching David — and the reader — that sex really isn't worth the time and effort, not to mention the risk. (Canadians have always felt this way, with some rare exceptions; see **Layton, Irving**.)

There are lots of other highlights in the mainly interior life of David Canaan. He forms a friendship with a buddy, Toby Richmond, but some lousy woman (Anna) gets in the way and ruins a good, old-fashioned male/male relationship. (For good, new-fashioned male/male relationships, see **Findley, Timothy** and **Tremblay, Michel**.) Finally David really gets off on farm work, cutting logs and moving rocks, when he could have just as easily been drawing water. (This is an example of "daring" in the book.) They also slaughter pigs, an activity thoroughly enjoyed by all, but David gets his hand ripped by a nail, one more example of the novel's profound Christian symbolism. David later falls off a scaffold, providing another example of Christian sloppiness in the book.

Toward the novel's end, both David's parents go off to that great Blue-nosed Kingdom in the sky, and his brother Chris leaves the farm, showing a common sense keenly lacking in the rest of the family. The novel concludes as it began, with David staring out the window, while his grandmother, now more than 200 years old, knits away like an old fool. But the book goes further, since Buckler felt that after several hundred pages, it was time for a little old Canadian action. David rushes from his beloved family farm and climbs the mountain he's been staring at, off and on, since page one. Foolishly he now dreams of becoming a wildly successful writer, when he really should have worked at becoming a decent mountain climber. He dies poetically and frigidly in the snow, without ever having shot a puck, drunk a beer or collected pogey. In other words, an unlived, if endlessly examined, Canadian life.

In a way, Ernest Buckler created, in *The Mountain and the Valley*, a sort of Canadianized, quick-frozen version of James Joyce's *A Portrait of the Artist as a Young Man*, with only a few minor differences: Buckler's book lacks excitement, drive, religious tension (other than the tension that comes from trying to figure out why David suffers like Christ while Christopher does not, when Christopher has the much more applicable name, and things like that), exterior action, Parnell and, of course, Dublin, making Buckler's Annapolis Valley seem like, well, like the Annapolis Valley. Still, if you consider an ancient grandmother knitting rugs, girls dying after lousy sex, and frustrated lives on the farm a source of thrills, then this is the book for you.

MORLEY CALLAGHAN

(1903 –)

MORLEY Callaghan is one of Canada's most respected and revered novelists and short story writers, because he was called that by the American critic Edmund Wilson in 1965, so it must be true. Born in Toronto to Irish Catholic parents, Callaghan attended Saint Michael's College at the University of Toronto, studying various arts subjects, but mainly boxing, so that he could beat the hell out of Hemingway and Fitzgerald in Paris several years later.

In 1923, Callaghan spent the summer working as a reporter for the *Toronto Star*. There he met Ernest Hemingway, who was then the European correspondent for the newspaper's weekly magazine, the *Star Weekly*. It was a momentous meeting, captured for posterity in both men's writings.

> *Hemingway's version*: There was this guy at the newspaper who tipped his hat to me.
> "Hello," he said.
> "Hello," I replied.

> *Callaghan's version*: I had gone along the crowded avenue, past the Catholic church, to the old building on King Street. Two tall maples towered over me as I saw the bearded, handsome man come out of the revolving front door.

> "Hello, Ernest," I said to the reporter, my mind swirling with Christian imagery, my feet soaking because I had foolishly, if not symbolically, forgotten my rubbers at home, which has no sexual reverberations whatsoever. "How *are* things, Ernie?"
>
> "How are ya doing, Morley?" the grinning man answered eagerly, delighted to run into a talented fellow writer in the heart of beautiful downtown Toronto. "How's the family? How's the writing going? Let's go out for a drink."
>
> In the distance, the white houses stood in rows, the clean streets forming patterns behind him; the cold breeze over the lake rustled my thinning hair, and Ernest grabbed my arm and joined me in the swirling, busy street.

As you can see, the two versions differed slightly, probably because Callaghan had once found a cache of adjectives in a drawer at the *Star*, which Hemingway had somehow mislaid.

In 1925, Callaghan received his B.A. in arts, enrolled in Osgoode Hall law school and began articling. In this he was also quite different from Hemingway, who would never use an article unless it was really necessary. But within a year, Callaghan's first short story was published in Paris, which was where it was at in the 1920s. Then more of his stories were published in Europe and the United States, making Callaghan far too important to waste his time doing unimportant, degrading things such as writing for the *Toronto Star* or working as a lawyer. (He had been called to the bar, but he never chose to practice, showing what a deeply moral Catholic he was.)

By 1928, Callaghan had been published three times in *Scribner's* magazine, and Maxwell Perkins, the legendary, yet true-to-life editor in New York, agreed to publish the young Canadian's first novel, *Strange Fugitive*, as well as a selection of his short stories. Indeed, Callaghan now began to be published in the Best Short Stories series in the U.S., appearing fourteen consecutive times. This, understandably, made him profoundly hated by every Canadian writer of his time, and for the next few decades to follow.

In 1929, Callaghan went off to Paris with his wife, where he spent much of his time with such famous expatriates as James Joyce, F. Scott Fitzgerald and fellow *Toronto Star*-hater Ernest Hemingway. For years after, Joyce, Fitzgerald and Hemingway used to regale their friends with stories of "what a great time we had with good old Morley Callaghan from Toronto." It was a time of great cafés, good wine, fond memories and namedropping like you wouldn't believe.

Just a few months later, The Torontonian Who Knew Joyce, Fitzgerald and Hemingway returned to Canada, with two complete novels, lots of short stories and enough recollections to write *That Summer in Paris* in 1963, just a third of a century after hobnobbing with the stars.

Back home, Callaghan turned out book after short story after book after short story, including *Such Is My Beloved* (1934), *They Shall Inherit the Earth* (1935) and *More Joy in Heaven* (**Mordecai Richler** might have described it as "More Goy in Heaven").

His major collection of short stories at this time was *Now That April's Here* (1937), but all his works during this period showed a growing concern for the tragic individual who longs to love and be loved, and to achieve recognition, yet just can't seem to adjust to society. (Sort of like Pierre Trudeau.) Another major concern was the terrible tension between material values and spiritual values. (Sort of like Jim and Tammy Faye Bakker — this was a writer ahead of his time.)

While waiting to be discovered by some American critic or other, Morley Callaghan had to make a living, so he wrote plays and essays, penned scripts for the National Film Board and moderated shows on CBC Radio. Perhaps the highlight of his career (including his summer with Joyce, Fitzgerald and Hemingway) was when he was a panelist on CBC's radio quiz show "Beat the Champs," and made regular appearances on Nathan Cohen's TV show "Fighting Words." All this involvement in the mass media was *supposed* to increase his book sales, but we know what Canada is like. The fools at the bookstores kept putting his novels and short story collections in the Canadiana section, which was the kiss of death.

Finally, in 1951, a potentially big breakthrough came: Callaghan published *The Loved and the Lost*, a novel that won a Governor General's Award. Alas, it was another kiss of death, so this book didn't sell well, either. Indeed, he even was awarded the revered Lorne Pierce Medal for distinguished contribution to Canadian literature, yet another kiss of death. Every Canadian writer must have at least nine lives if he wants to eventually succeed in this country.

Finally, in 1965, the Big Breakthrough came to Morley Callaghan. The great critic Edmund Wilson described the Canadian writer as "the most unjustly neglected novelist in the English-speaking world" and compared him with Chekhov and Turgenev. Canadian critics scratched their heads over the latter names, but they did go back and pick up Callaghan's recently published memoirs, in which he wrote about Fitzgerald and Hemingway. Now *those* were guys they had heard of.

Callaghan finally earned some respect, having honorary doctorates bestowed upon him, Canada Council Medals and prizes thrust upon him and, in June, 1970, the real honour: the $50,000 Royal Bank Award. Now that was the kind of respect his fellow Canadians could relate to.

Over the past two decades, Toronto's Morley Callaghan has continued to put out new novels on a far more regular schedule than most writers over the age of seventy or eighty. Most Canadian authors have long since starved to death by that age.

THE PLOT OF *SUCH IS MY BELOVED* (1934)

LONG BEFORE NEWFOUNDLAND made the subject topical, we encounter Stephen Dowling, an eager young priest who finds himself drawn to two young women of easy virtue. (Actually, since these were *women* the priest was getting involved with, maybe it was topical at the time.)

The priest, wearing a scarf, is accosted by the women, who, unable to see his collar, are unaware of Father Dowling's vow of celibacy. Indeed, the word *celibacy* is utterly unknown to both Ronnie and Midge. The priest talks himself into believing that these women need his love as much as everyone else in the parish, ignoring the salient fact that it's not the kind of love these babes are usually interested in. Now, if God's love paid $2 for fifteen minutes, maybe, but otherwise, that's about it.

The novel consists of this great tension between sacred and secular love, with most of the characters, and frequently the reader, believing that the priest is a dirty young man, while the two streetwalkers keep waiting for him to put up or shut up. Father Dowling spends all his money buying the women clothes, including the money he normally sends to his elderly mother, who hasn't been well enough to walk the streets for many years.

A climax is reached — don't worry, this is a thirties novel, not an eighties one — when Father Dowling is transferred to another parish by his bishop, who also tells the cops to transfer the two floozies to another parish, as well. This so unhinges the young priest (along with the reader, who's been waiting for the Good Parts for over a hundred pages) that he becomes deranged and is sent to a mental institution. The moral is clear: if you hang around with whores and never get around to doing it, the frustration can drive you nuts, especially if you are a man of God. Amen.

FROM *THAT SUMMER IN PARIS* *(1963)*

HOW YA DOIN' SCOTT?" I asked Fitzgerald, the author of *The Great Gatsby* and so many other fine books.

"I'm okay, Morley," said Scott, grinning handsomely at this Canadian author of several fine short stories and a novel that Maxwell Perkins really liked a lot.

"Hi!" said Hemingway, smashing his way in through the locked front door of my Parisian apartment. He was always a man of few words, both in real life and in his several admired novels, the names of which I forget just now.

Suddenly Picasso burst through the shattered door and began painting stunning pictures of bulls and naked women all over my living room wall.

"Oh, cut the crap, Pablo!" exploded Ernest, emitting the longest sentence I've ever heard come from his mouth. "Why don't we go boxing?"

"Boxing Day isn't till the day after Christmas," I mumbled, ever the Canadian.

"Every day is Boxing Day in Paris!" cried Scott, who

marched toward the door, pulling his coat off the sleeping body of the fine English author Ford Madox Ford before grabbing James Joyce by the arm — he'd been in my kitchen, cooking up some Irish whiskey — and heading for the club.

When we got there, Ernest couldn't wait to climb into the ring. "Time!" shouted Scott, as he grabbed a watch away from Joan (pronounced Juan) Miro, the fine painter. I joined Hemingway in the ring, pushing aside Georges Braque, who had been painting stupid cubes all over the back of my trunks.

Ernest could hardly wait for the fight to begin. He lunged forward with the first insult.

"It gets so cold in Toronto, an exhibitionist once came up to me and described himself,"* Hemingway spewed, almost knocking me to the canvas.

I stepped back and let him have it. "You Americans are so dumb, you think de Tocqueville is spelled with a 'k.'" Blood spurted from Hemingway's lower lip as he scowled at me, clearly hurt.

"*Oh, yeah*, Morley?" Ernest sneered. "It's so cold in your godforsaken home town, I once came out of the *Star* building and saw a Greyhound bus with the greyhound riding on the inside."

I collapsed to the canvas, my ear half torn off by his horrible statement. I thought I saw Vincent Van Gogh in the distance, but it was only his ear that I imagined; it was really Jimmy Joyce, singing an Irish lullaby and winking at me through his thick glasses. What a sweet voice he had, like an angel. But I never could understand a damn thing he wrote.

---

* Scholars have noted that Hemingway must have read the early Canadian author Frances Brooke.

"I've had enough of boxing," exclaimed Scott Fitzgerald, as each of us pulled on our jackets and marched out into the coolish Parisian evening.

"Let's go hear Josephine Baker," I suggested.

"Naw, let's hop over to Gertie Stein's," Scott insisted.

"Are you nuts?" Hemingway sneered. "Baker's a Negro and Stein's a Jew. Why don't we . . . " He looked around in a panic, his face white as a sheet. "Where the hell are we?" Ernest gasped in horror. "I don't even know where we are!"

"You know, neither do I," whispered Scotty, equally concerned.

"But of course." I grinned in my disarmingly Canadian fashion. "We're the lost generation — remember?"

WILFRED CAMPBELL

(1858 – 1918)

CAMPBELL was born in Berlin, but this didn't help his German sales much — it was Berlin, Ontario, later renamed Kitchener. He was the son of an Anglican clergyman who had moved from parish to parish to (perish the thought) parish, right across eastern Ontario and Georgian Bay, looking for people who had not yet heard his single sermon.

It was in these many towns that young Wilfred began to write his romantic poetry. Not *that* romantic, however, since he would soon attend Wycliffe College of the University of Toronto and a theological school in New England, before returning to Canada to preach. This time it would be St. Stephen, New Brunswick, that would hear the single sermon of a new generation of Campbells.

While in the United States, Campbell became interested

in mythology and transcendentalism, demonstrating that the church could have problems with its ministers even back then. Campbell feared animal and nature worship, and fought against them by writing poems that worshipped nature and animals. He left the ministry in 1891 and entered the Civil Service in Ottawa, a city where even his one tedious sermon seemed exciting. But he spent all his leisure time — which means all his time, since the Civil Service in Ottawa was the same back then as it is today — writing poems about such still relevant topics as the lakes of Canada (now dead), the ideals of the British race (a race lost in the 1950s in the world and in the 1960s in Canada) and the future of man (which eventually became the future of civilization, then women, in the 1970s and 1980s).

Campbell also wrote hundreds of novels, travel books, poetic dramas and articles for countless magazines, often earning a few dollars. Over the years he held positions, as opposed to working, in the Department of Railways and Canals (this was when Canada still had both), the Department of Militia and Defence (ditto, ditto), the Privy Council Office (where he spent most of his time in the privy) and the Public Archives (which was just as private). A committed Imperialist at a time when it was not considered that imperialists needed to be committed, he wept longer over the death of Queen Victoria than Albert would have. Campbell eventually died in Ottawa, which is nothing new.

BLISS CARMAN

(1861 – 1929)

BORN in Fredericton, Bliss Carman spent most of his fruitful life telling people he was related — "First cousins!" he'd squeal — to Charles G. D.

Roberts. When this ploy failed to get the girls interested, he would mention that both he and Ralph Waldo Emerson had the same great-great-grandfather. This didn't work, either, especially with potential publishers, so he just had to depend on his looks, which were a knockout.

Like his first cousin, Bliss Carman went to the University of New Brunswick, before studying in Edinburgh for several years, where he learned where all the important Canadians of the nineteenth century came from. He returned to Canada and considered a career in law. But Carman had too much common sense, honesty and self-respect for that. Then he considered engineering, but realized there were never any girls in that school. And they wouldn't have known who Emerson was, anyway. Or Charles G. D. Roberts.

And so, Carman went to Harvard, where he studied philosophy, better known in the 1880s as "Unemployment 101." He met a young poet there and they worked on several books together, and during the last decade of that century, he wrote for and edited various American magazines. Some of his most famous poems were written at this time, many of them even getting published, which was the whole point.

For the next three decades, Carman wrote poem after poem after poem whenever he was inspired, and even more often when he wasn't.

Like so many Canadians, Carman was moved and inspired by his country's glowing nature and beauty, even though it was winter most of the time. So he started living way down in the deep south of the United States — Connecticut — each winter, and in the Catskills in the summer. Not being Jewish or particularly funny, except unintentionally, he never did make it in the latter, although he knocked 'em dead in New England on several occasions, especially at readings.

In 1925, Bliss Carman got tired of the rat race in Connecticut and the Catskills (he kept betting on the wrong rat and lost almost his entire inheritance), and chose to return to Canada, where he was known and respected. He began to do recitals, and searched out more lakes to eulogize and trees to fondle. There was an abundance of both.

Carman was now honoured by his countrymen with oodles of literary awards, if not a knighthood, since he didn't live long enough to earn one for Not Having Starved to Death from a Long Career in Canadian Literature. He passed away in Connecticut, which is a helluva lot better than dying in the Catskills, something George Burns and so many others did during the same years Carman was there. He at least died in New Canaan, which was more than Moses ever accomplished. Carman's ashes, no longer filled with bliss, were taken up to Fredericton, however, and had no trouble crossing the border for one (inarguably) last time.

Although Carman never married, he did live with a woman for the last thirty years of his life. She was also his patron, an arrangement we heartily recommend to every struggling artist. (When he told her that he was related to Ralph Waldo Emerson, she was wowed for life, if not for marriage.) And unlike so many poets in history, he *did* live long enough to be greatly honoured: he was considered a kind of unofficial poet laureate of Canada, even though he was more than willing to have it made official. Just before his death, he received the Lorne Pierce Medal for service to literature, which did him little good, and honorary degrees from both his Maritime alma mater and McGill, which did him even less good. He also received a posthumous medal from the Poetry Society of America, which did him absolutely no good whatsoever, since he was unable to live to see it, though this is the whole idea of posthumous awards, when you think about it. You can visit his grave in Fredericton, where he is more than likely still churning out poetry — he wrote over four dozen volumes during his lifetime, and had made threats to a number of critics before he died that he had no intention whatsoever of letting his passing stop him. Death was not proud, and neither was Carman.

His poems were surprisingly good, especially the handful of really well-written ones. What Carman needed was an editor — actually, what he needed was a chain saw. His primary problem (see **Layton, Irving**) was that he tended to repeat himself, be redundant, become repetitive and say the same thing over and over and over. Again. And again.

See the following. Below. Just underneath this line. Down there. Coming next. Okay, already.

From *Low Tide on Grand Pré* *(1893)*

The sun drops down like butterscotch
    It sloshes over rushing tide
And Nature never makes a botch
    I know that I shall never hide
While waiting for the coming tide.

Was it last year, or long ago?
    We smoked the grass we grew out back,
And reached new highs — if sometimes low
    And if arrested, took the flak,
But hid New Brunswick Gold out back.

The sex was great, or so I think,
    For I'm not sure that I remember —
We saw a rabbit, or maybe mink,
    But I am *sure* it was November,
Or then again, was it September?

The night has come, so too the tide —
    It's finally high, or maybe low,
It's hard to tell when I am high
    But then again, my mind is slow,
I think I should have just said "no."

ROCH CARRIER

(1937 –)

ONE of the most accessible of all Québécois writers, mainly because Anglo readers are happy to read him in English, Roch Carrier was born in a tiny village in Quebec called Ste-Justine-de-Dorchester, which we trust has since had its name changed to Ste-Justine-de-Lévesque. After studying at the Université de Montréal and the Sorbonne, Carrier began a long career in teaching, writing a series of disarming novels since 1964. Overflowing with stupid English characters who appealed greatly to his French readers, these included the highly successful *La Guerre, yes sir!* (1968), brilliantly translated into *La Guerre, Yes Sir!* two years later, a title that would not appear in Quebec bookstores in the 1990s, either inside or outside the window.

Carrier's most successful short story was *The Hockey Sweater* (1979). It was not only turned into a delightful NFB cartoon, but also became a beautifully illustrated children's book. The tale touched all its readers with its powerful sense of reality and truth: after all, what Québécois child would want to wear a Toronto Maple Leaf sweater? Come to think of it, until the fluke 1989/90 NHL season, what professional hockey player would want to wear a Toronto Maple Leaf sweater?

LEONARD COHEN

(1934 –   )

ONE of the Montreal Jewish mafia, which pretty well includes most English-speaking writers from that city, Leonard Cohen was born in 1934 and grew up in the affluent Westmount area many years before the boys from the Main sold enough books to move there. Educated at McGill University, he published his first book of poetry, *Let Us Compare Mythologies*, in 1956. In fact, he wrote most of the poems between the ages of fifteen and twenty, when most other kids his age were still checking for zits.

After a three-week attempt to do graduate studies at Columbia University in New York, Cohen returned in defeat to Montreal. There he read poems in nightclubs,

wrote unpublishable novels and even worked briefly in the family clothing business. That experience led to one of his most famous poems, "Maria/please find me/I am almost 38 long."

In 1961, Cohen had his first major literary success, *The Spice-Box of Earth.* Literary success in poetry, of course, means more than 500 copies sold. The collection was not only heavily Jewish in subject matter — already pretty exotic for Canada in the early 1960s — but was filled with lyrics about love, when 90 percent of this country's poetry until that time had been about icebergs moving down from Baffin Island and grizzlies arguing with beavers. The only previous poems about the birds and the bees had described them freezing to death in the bush.

After spending a few years in England, where he spoke the language so well, he published his first novel, *The Favorite Game*, and eventually moved to the island of Hydra, off Greece, where the weather was more than 750 percent better than on the island of Montreal, in the St. Lawrence. Make that 1,000 percent better. A lot fewer family clothing stores, too.

Not only did Cohen write another successful novel, *Beautiful Losers* (1966), making the characters "I" and "F" famous across Canada (at least initially), he went on to turn out several more popular collections of poetry, including *Flowers for Hitler* (1964), *Parasites of Heaven* (1966), *Death of a Lady's Man* (1978) and more. Alas, he became a much loved singer/songwriter during this period, as well, recording such best-selling albums as *Songs of Leonard Cohen*, *Songs from a Room*, *Songs of Love and Hate*, *New Skin for the Old Ceremony*, et al. All his songs showed a striking poetic ability, and were performed in a voice that eerily resembled Bob Dylan's, with laryngitis. Over the years, Cohen regularly visited his native Montreal — "to renew [his] neurotic affiliations," to quote the witty poet — and in the past decade, chose to return permanently to that city, if not to his talents.

Muse, please find him. He'll soon be pushing sixty.

SUZANNE

Suzanne takes you down
To her place by the river
You can see her shop is open,
But she cannot claim "DELIVER"
Since the signs of course are in French
For although Suzanne speaks English
And her clientele is Anglo
She must have her sign *en français*
'Cause this is *la belle province*
And that's how those things are done here . . . .
And you want to go and shop there
And you want to buy some blinds
But you cannot figure out the words —
For they've touched your purse and pocket with
their signs.

Jesus was a salesman
And he had a store to sell in
But he knew he'd better speak French
No more English could he yell in
For the government in Quebec
Had made its feelings clear
That all signs must be *en français*
Both in front and in the rear . . . .
But you want to shop in English
And you want to read the words

But the PQ and the Liberals
Have said that English rights are for the birds.

FROM *BEAUTIFUL LOSERS*
(1966)

GOD IS AHEAD. Magic is afoot. God is ahead. Magic is afoot. God is afoot. Magic is ahead. My horse is behind. His horse is ahead. God costs an arm and a leg. Baking soda is arm and hammer. Look at the legs on that chick. God never sickened, but McClelland and Stewart is always in trouble. Many politicians lied. Many potatoes fried. Not enough politicians died. Magic never weakened, but the CBC always did. God never died, but he hasn't been too healthy in this century. God was ruler, but he wasn't afoot, he was a yard. Magic was afoot, which isn't metric, either. Many men bled, but women do it more naturally. Magic always led, but to turn gold to lead is what it's all about. Many stones rolled, but the Rolling Stones go on forever. Many fat men questioned, but the Thin Man knew the answer. Magic was fed, but God wasn't dead. You load sixteen tons and what do you get: another day older and deeper in debt. God rules. Coles rules. Smith rules. Classics once ruled, but now Smith and Coles rule the roost. Roosters crow. A lot of men didn't and a lot of men died. Magic is the end. God is the beginning. Is this the beginning or the end? Is this is the beginning of the end? Is this the promised end? (*King Lear*, Act V, Scene iii). Magic is no instrument. A flute is an instrument. My voice is an instrument, although it sure as hell sounds out of tune. The police arrested Magic, but Magic would not tarry; he sued for false arrest, won his case, big bucks, and moved to the

Eastern Townships. Magic cannot come to harm. Harm, Manitoba, is no longer reached by the CPR, making the railroad out of Harm's way. Weak men lied. Sick men died. They died of athlete's foot, which is afoot yet still near at hand. The mountains danced for they had heard that God was dead. But as long as there are televangelists, God will never die. Magic exists as long as English is spoken in Quebec, which doesn't look too promising; I'd take out insurance if I were Magic. Magic is moving through the world, and the mind is Magic and the flesh is Magic, as Irving Layton has been reminding Canadians for half a century. Magic dances on a clock, but does anybody know what time it is, does anybody really care? And to think that if I had remained in the family clothing business, Magic would never have been alive, God never afoot and the hip bone would still be attached to the knee bone. Let's call the whole thing off.

JOHN ROBERT COLOMBO

(1936 –)

ALTHOUGH the Kitchener-born poet has edited *Tamarack Review*, taught school, written book reviews, edited and anthologized several dozen books (including the seminal *Colombo's Canadian Quotations* in 1974 and *Colombo's Canadian References* in 1976), he has gone on to publish several thousand more books that make one worry about him, such as *Colombo's Canadian Matchboxes* (1983), *Colombo's Canadian Used Mufflers* (1986), *Colombo's Canadian Microwave Ovens* (1988) and *Colombo's Favourite Remaindered Books* (every year). Still, while he seems to spread himself, as well as his numerous publishers' reckless advances, a bit thin, he is most fondly remembered for the often impressive "found poetry" of his youth, an example of which appears below.

Lost and Found
(1966)

Transfer: Bathurst Bus 7C
Milk Cheese Eggs Butter Campbell's Soup
Men's shirt, launder — no starch
Theo, clean your goddam room today or you
can forget about the hockey game this week
Jack McClelland called, darling, and wants
you to stop calling him anymore
WALK DON'T WALK WALK DON'T
WALK WALK DON'T WALK
Ruth, don't wait up for me; I went out for a
long WALK
DON'T WALK WALK DON'T WALK
Campbell's Soup, 29c

Ralph Connor
(1860 – 1937)

His real name was Charles William Gordon, and like most best-selling Canadian writers in our history, he was a Presbyterian minister. Writing more than two dozen novels, known poetically by his millions of fans as "penny dreadfuls" (unlike today, when most Canadian novels are "twenty-four-ninety-five dreadfuls"), Connor/Gordon turned out books faster than he turned out drunks from St. Stephen's Church outside Winnipeg, where he served for more than four decades while simultaneously penning novels. His favourite declaration during this period was "I'd love to officiate at that funeral, but I've got to go over the galleys of *Black Rock/The Sky Pilot/The Foreigner*," etc., etc.

His greatest success was *The Man from Glengarry* (1901), a frontier book about a man named Ranald Macdonald, who, in spite of his name, was no clown. Like all best-selling books of the time (he sold *five million copies of his first three books*, a fact that tends to make most contemporary Canadian writers green with envy), the book is overflowing with disarmingly racist Scottish, Irish and French-Canadian dialects, not to mention derelicts. The goal of the title character is to civilize the West and make it part of the rest of the country, something Pierre Trudeau utterly failed to accomplish (and his books on federalism didn't sell beans, either). Ultimately, the most attractive thing about Connor/Gordon today is that he never claimed he was a writer. Would that many of our so-called writers today were so brutally honest.

ISABELLA VALANCY CRAWFORD

(1850 – 1887)

ALTHOUGH Crawford lived for less than four decades, most critics are astounded by how much awful poetry she managed to churn out in such a brief time. Few, however, feel that had she reached the Biblical three-score-and-ten years, her writing would have gotten much better.

Isabella Valancy Crawford was born in Dublin, Ireland, one of eleven children, of whom not one, apparently, showed any talent whatsoever. Her father, hearing of the fine quality of the whiskey in the New World, took his four surviving children to Upper Canada in 1858, when Isabella was eight. She never learned English.

In the village of Paisley in Bruce County, Ontario, her father practised medicine, bartering his services for food from the farmers in the area. Reportedly, Crawford got the better deal.

The family later moved to Lakefield, Ontario, where **Margaret Laurence** would, still later, prove that good writing in the area was possible. Interestingly, the Crawford clan first stayed in the house of a nephew of **Susanna Moodie** and **Catharine Parr Traill**, suggesting just how few Canadians there were during this era. The family was impoverished — an impossibility for today's doctors — and eventually, Ms. Crawford's father was convicted of mishandling public funds while serving as the treasurer of the tiny town of Paisley. She needed some way to bring pride back to her devastated family. Why not write bad poetry to take revenge upon the society that had treated her loved ones so poorly?

Soon after, Isabella and her mother moved to Toronto, and lived above a grocery store in the downtown area. Fittingly, no plaque is on the wall of that building today. The young woman wrote short stories, poems and novels, most of which she was kind enough not to publish. The one book of verse that appeared during her lifetime was put out at her own expense, and was remaindered in hours. In fact, only about four dozen copies of the 1,000 printed were ever sold. (This percentage of books sold continues in Canadian poetry to this day.) It was called *Old Spookses' Pass, Malcolm's Katie and Other Poems* (1884), although few critics called it anything at all. And so, when Isabella Valancy Crawford died of heart failure in 1887, it wasn't her first failure. Yet, only three-quarters of a century after her death, Canadian theatre critic Nathan Cohen described her plays as "at the most charitably, incompetent," marking one of the few times he was ever so kind to an author.

FROM *MALCOLM'S KATIE*

Uuga! Uuga! Shame on you, O Pale Face!
And shame on you, O moon of evil spirits!
Have you murdered the joyous, laughing Summer?
Have you killed the mummy of the flowers?
Stop your icy spells of lousy weather!
No more ghosts of all the slaughtered flowers —
Linger with your spring and kiss the branches
Linger touching all the loving places
Naked, nude and bare, they*

ROBERTSON DAVIES

(1913 –)

BORN in Thamesville, Ontario, which will be far better remembered as the Deptford of his later novels, Robertson Davies came into the world severely disadvantaged: he was not from a tiny Manitoba town, like **Margaret Laurence**; he did not hang around St. Urbain Street with hostile Jewish children of immigrants, like **Mordecai Richler**; he did not come from England, Scotland or Ireland, like **Stephen Leacock** and half the Canadian writers of the previous century. He had only a father who was a senator and the owner and publisher of the Kingston *Whig-Standard*. Clearly Davies

* Author's note: My lawyer has warned me not to print any more of Isabella Valancy Crawford's poetry in this book. Not because it is in public domain or that I can be sued, but simply because my lawyer is a lover of good poetry.

would have to make it on his own, studying at Upper Canada College and Queen's University, hacking it through Balliol College, Oxford, and working at the Old Vic in England. It's never easy to be born with a silver fork in your mouth, and when you're also a member of an ethnic charter group, this has been known to be fatal to talent.

But not for Davies, who, even though he was such a disaster in mathematics he had to be admitted to Queen's as a "special student," managed to land difficult-to-get jobs such as working on the editorial staff of the Peterborough *Examiner*, which his father also owned. Indeed, he worked his way up to the role of editor and owner, with his two brothers, by 1946. Making it in Canada is always open to those who work hard at it, even if they get rejected for war service along the way.

It was only after the war that Davies began to turn out books based on the column he had been writing for the *Examiner*, under the pseudonym "Samuel Marchbanks." *The Diary of Samuel Marchbanks* (1947) and *The Table Talk of Samuel Marchbanks* (1949) showed him to be a sharp critic of Canadian manners of the time, when most Canadians hadn't even realized they had any. During this same period he wrote countless plays, each more awful than the next, moving his many fans to pray that he would turn to poetry, painting, bankrobbery, *anything*.

He did. With his three Salterton novels — *Tempest-Tost* (1951), *Leaven of Malice* (1954) and *A Mixture of Frailties* (1958) — he chose to satirize a small university city in Ontario, clearly modelled after Kingston. Kingston was scandalized, and the rest of the country couldn't see what there was there to satirize: everyone over the age of ten knew that Canadians were provincial, second-rate and boring, especially those who came from one-horse, one-university towns like Salterton/Kingston.

Meanwhile, Davies was involved in the young Stratford Festival, serving on its board for almost all of its first two decades. He moved to Toronto in 1963 to become Master of Massey College at the University of Toronto, where things were still provincial, second-rate and boring, although there were a number of universities around to make things more interesting than Salterton/Kingston.

Davies achieved international fame with the publication of his Deptford Trilogy, even captivating countless readers in the United States, whose attention can usually only be captured by horror fiction, pornography or attacks on actresses by their daughters. Once again, with *Fifth Business* (1970), *The Manticore* (1972) and *World of Wonders* (1975), Davies now showed the world that Canada is a country lacking in spirituality and overflowing in materialism. In spite of this, Davies decided to keep all the money that poured in from his best-selling books. Still, as the first Canadian ever to be made an honorary member of the American Academy of Arts and Letters, Robertson Davies has now truly gained the respect and admiration of his fellow Canadians, in spite of their materialism and shallow spirituality, and also in spite of his Lorne Pierce Medal (1961) and his being made a Companion of the Order of

Canada (1972). Hell, if the Yanks think he's a great novelist, that's good enough for us.

The Complete Plot of the Deptford Trilogy in One Paragraph

PERCY BOYD STAUNTON, aka Boy, throws a snowball with a stone hidden inside it at his ten-year-old Deptford friend, Dunstan Ramsay, who is really called Dunstable, but the names are already confusing enough. Ramsay ducks, making the snowball hit Mary Dempster, who is pregnant by her husband, who is a minister but not Catholic, so it's okay. The accident pushes Mary into early labour, but she and her infant, Paul Dempster, are nursed back to health by Dunstan's mother, who cautions the new mother against ever getting stoned again while pregnant. Dunstan alone knows that Boy (and a naughty boy he was, too) had thrown the snowball, but he never lets anyone know because of his decency and sense of honour, not to mention Boy's threats to cut his little throat. But as Mary Dempster sinks into insanity — often the only sensible way to escape a small Ontario town — Dunstan feels profound guilt. He feels even worse when the crazed Mary is discovered making whoopie with a bum in a pit outside town, shocking and horrifying the townspeople and moving her sensitive, kindly minister husband, Amasa Dempster, to do the only proper thing an Ontario religious leader can do to a promiscuous, lunatic wife: tie her to a bedpost with a rope. Still, there is some goodness even in the corrupt and the insane, as any follower of Canadian politics knows so well, and when Dunstan's brother Willie nearly dies, it is Mary Dempster who nurses him back to health, without even asking for his provincial health insurance number. Along comes the Great War, which really wasn't so great (see

Findley, Timothy), and Dunstan wins the Victoria Cross, which is only one of many crosses he'll have to bear. Never forgetting the woman who got stoned in his place, Dunstan sends money to help her after her husband and aunt die, and after her son Paul vanishes, only to return many hundreds of pages later in another guise — but we're getting ahead of ourselves. Eventually, Mary Dempster dies in a Toronto hospital for crazy people. Boy Staunton, in the meantime, has returned from the war (see **Findley**) and makes big bucks expanding in his father's business (see **Newman, Peter C.**), forming a major corporation, while keeping his friendship with Dunstan and occasionally assisting with a little insider trading. Boy marries the childhood sweetheart of both of them, Leola Cruikshank, who bears his two beautiful children and lives with him in a magnificent mansion. This inevitably means that she chooses to try to kill herself and ends up dying of pneumonia, being a Canadian who just can't stand such success. Boy's daughter Caroline goes ahead and marries a wimp, while David becomes a successful lawyer, which means that he must become a drunk and try Jungian analysis in Zurich, since it obviously worked so well for Robertson Davies. Dunstan, on the other hand, has come back from the war missing a leg, something that pretty well rules out the 1920 Olympics, but there is at least some good news awaiting him upon his return to Canada: both his parents have died in the flu epidemic, leaving the readers with at least two fewer characters to keep track of. It is clear that Dunstan must escape from his home town, if only on one leg, which now seems inevitable. He obtains his M.A. in history and begins to teach at Colborne College, a prep school near Toronto, where, inevitably, Boy is a governor, since it's a small world and this is a small country in spite of its large geography. Indeed, Dunstan actually gets to teach David

Staunton, proving that this really *is* a small world. It's a small continent, too, for as Dunstan travels across Europe and spends some time in Mexico, he keeps running into Paul Dempster, the son of crazy Mary and the same kid who was from his mother's womb untimely ripp'd, all because of that damned snowball back in the first line. Of course, this being a Robertson Davies novel, Paul goes under the name of Jules Le Grand, and while in Mexico he is called Magnus Eisengrim. Le Grand/Eisengrim has now become a great magician, with a worldwide fame, which only goes to show you just how important it is to get out of Canada (see Greene, Lorne; Fox, Michael J.; Jennings, Peter and several million more). The magician, who now has a Swiss business partner with the NHL-hockey-player name of Liesl Vitzliputzli requests Dunstan's assistance in ghostwriting a phony autobiography of Le Grand/Eisengrim to be sold at his shows along with popcorn and candy (see Drabinsky, Garth. On second thought, don't). Interestingly, since everyone runs into everyone else sooner or later in their lives if they're from a small Ontario town, Boy doesn't recognize Magnus as Paul when Dunstan brings the two together at Colborne College. Boy doesn't even remember throwing that stone, even when Dunstan brings it out of his pocket, along with the ashes of Mary Dempster, which is pretty grotesque when you think about it. The stone strangely vanishes from the room, but it is fortunately found later that night in the mouth of the dead Boy Staunton, who has raced his car into Lake Ontario — another highly recommended way to escape the stultification of living in a small Ontario town. Dunstan feels terrible about the rather ugly death of Boy, and now feels guilty about arranging that meeting between him and Paul/Le Grand/Magnus. In fact, he feels so bad about it, he has a heart attack during a performance of the great magician —

one of the sleaziest examples of upstaging a performer in the annals of show business. (It didn't help that David Staunton had screamed out from the cheaper seats at this performance, "WHO KILLED BOY STAUNTON?" which utterly confused everyone in the audience, including those who had read the first book of the trilogy.) Clearly upset, since having a father drive his car into Lake Ontario with a killer stone in his mouth is one of the worst guilt trips a parent can lay upon a child, young David Staunton heads off to begin analysis with Johanna von Haller at the Jung Institute in Zurich, where he learns much about life, without ever having to read a Davies novel. Then another wonderful coincidence occurs: David Staunton meets up with Dunstan Ramsay and Liesl Vitzliputzli, who has, unfortunately, still not changed her name, and is finally introduced to the great magician Magnus, which helps young David to free himself from his family guilt far better than months of analysis, Jungian or otherwise. We now shift to the perspective of Paul Dempster/Jules Le Grand/ Magnus Eisengrim, who retells the events of his life in order to get a part in a BBC film, obviously because CBC, as always, never seems to express any interest in its most illustrious citizens. We are delighted to relive the agonizing life of Dempster in Deptford, his birth, his kidnapping and his sexual molestation by a magician named Willard in an itinerant circus show, something far too many Canadians can personally identify with, especially in small towns. But Magnus somehow triumphs over his painful childhood, becoming a world-famous magician, sort of like Robertson Davies. Of course, it didn't hurt to have a grotesquely deformed, apelike but exceedingly wealthy woman named Vitzliputzli, named after one of the demons called up by Faust in Goethe's nearly-as-long play, to help Paul Dempster/Le Grand/Eisengrim along the way. I hope you have this all straight. I'm not making this up, you know.

MAZO DE LA ROCHE

(1879 – 1961)

THE writer who almost singlehandedly ruined CBC-TV, although it wasn't her fault, because she was already dead, was born in 1879 in a town just north of Toronto. She was an only child, who was shipped off to Galt, and even a fruit farm near Bronte, as well as a cottage near Clarkson. This would create for her a vision of rural life that she would rub in the eyes of her countless readers for the next half century.

In 1894, still a young teenager, Mazo Roche (which is what her real name was, and you've got to admit "De La Roche" has a certain *je ne sais quoi* that was lacking before) met her cousin Caroline Clement, whom she would eventually somehow "adopt" and live with for the rest of her life. Indeed, they even adopted two children.

By 1915, her short stories were appearing in such periodicals as the *Atlantic Monthly* — pretty impressive for a strange, eccentric woman who was stuck eternally in Victorian Ontario. Over the next decade she turned out several novels that were a lot like Bronte. Unfortunately we mean Bronte, Ontario, where she had spent part of her youth; she never could write as well as the Bronte sisters, you can be sure of that.

Then an event transpired that changed De La Roche's life forever. She wrote a book called *Jalna* in 1927 that was so astonishingly popular she was cruelly forced to write fifteen sequels, pretty much destroying any last bit of creativity in her strange mind. But, then, if you had tossed off a book that sold 100,000 copies across the United States in three months you'd probably write fifteen sequels, too. Look at *Rocky* or *Nightmare on Elm Street*, and you'll get the idea.

Still, *Jalna* was a most impressive novel. After all, did it not sell 100,000 copies across the United States in just a few months? Who can forget the soldier Philip Whiteoak and his lovely bride, Adeline? Who can forget Adeline as "Gran," the voluptuous and demanding matriarch who rules Jalna until she is mercifully put to death at the age of 100 by Mazo De La Roche? Who can forget Renny, her driven, passionate grandson, who would finally take over Jalna after Gran's eventual, too-long-in-coming death? Who can forget Renny's love for the Yankee bride of Eden, his brother? Who can forget the bastard daughter of their neighbour, whom Eden makes love to and whom his brother Piers elopes with, saving us another endless description of a wedding? Who can forget their parrot, which swears in foreign languages, not unlike the readers who somehow got hooked on this godforsaken series (over ten million copies sold in hardcover; eat your heart out, Pierre)? Who can forget the 1935 movie version of *Jalna*? Who can forget the miserable CBC-TV series of 1972, which was so awful it inspired mass migration from various parts of Canada to Nicaragua, Panama and Lebanon?

Actually, this writer did, and had to look up all the above in various books.

Still, Mazo De La Roche managed to have it all during her long lifetime: a loving companion, two children, more than a dozen monster best-sellers, movies made of her books and a death that came kindly — and early enough to spare her from having to watch the CBC-TV series. And if her descriptions of life and love in early twentieth-century Ontario prevented tens of millions of readers from ever wanting to migrate to this obviously wealthy, rural country, that's not De La Roche's fault. She was only out to entertain — a lot more than can be said for a good number of the writers profiled in this book.

William Henry Drummond

(1854 – 1907)

"Unwild Bill" Drummond was born in Ireland and, being only ten at the time, chose to come with his parents to Canada, in spite of their protestations. He studied to be a doctor and practised in rural Quebec, where he preceded Eaton's by more than a quarter century in his savage insistence that any French-Canadian patient "speak English, godammit."

During his life, Drummond wrote countless poems of both the "nondialect" and "dialect" variety. Because we Canadians have such a great sense of humour, not to mention a great passion for condescending racism, only the latter were very popular. His first collection, *The Habitant and Other French-Canadian Poems* (1897), was wildly successful, which says more about the Canadian public at the time than about Drummond's talents. It was only after his death by a stroke (and not by the hand of an offended *habitant*, in spite of what some scholars have suggested), that readers discovered Drummond's medical work had been done primarily in Montreal and his country work almost entirely among Scottish people, rather than the Québécois. Ergo, his poems capture the reality of French-Canadian *habitant* life with the same keen exactitude as Shakespeare captured Italian life in *Romeo and Juliet* and ancient Roman life in *Julius Caesar*.

In many ways Drummond's poems are the literary equivalent of Cornelius Krieghoff's nineteenth-century paintings of the *habitant*, with the minor difference that Krieghoff was gifted and that Ken Thomson wouldn't even think of collecting poems by William Henry Drummond.

Still, the poet's *habitant* works continue to be widely studied and memorized by unruly and uninterested school children from Newfoundland to British Columbia. The Québécois know better. Indeed, several hundred thousand French Canadians signed petitions in the late 1980s, requesting that the right to "opt out of studying Drummond's poems" be included in the Meech Lake Accord.

FROM *THE WRECK OF THE JULIE PLANTE*
(1897)

'Twas a dark night on Lac Saint Trudeau
  Dat wind did blow, blow, blow
An' de crew of dat boat, der *Julie Plante*,
  Got fear'd an' run down low —
For de win' she blasted really fierce
  And den she blew lots more!
And de cap'n he did hit his head
  Upon dat mast

LOUIS DUDEK
(1918 –   )

BORN in Montreal to Polish immigrant parents, which was no crime in that city back in those days, unlike today, Louis Dudek studied at McGill, then worked as a copywriter for an advertising firm, something that shows in much of his poetry. Indeed, the eye-catching and enticing nature of the titles of most of his poetry collections shows just how successful an ad man he was: *East of the City* (1946), *Twenty-four Poems* (1952), *Europe* (1955), *En Mexico* (1958), *Collected Poetry* (1971), *Selected Poems* (1979), *Cross-section* (1980) and *Continuation* (1981) are just a few of the most exciting ones. Compare this with **Pierre Berton**'s *Fast Fast Fast Relief*, and you'll get an idea of which writer was more commercial.

During the 1940s and 1950s, Dudek edited some very important poetry reviews, including *First Statement*, *Northern Review* and *Contact*, and was profoundly involved with the small press movement in Canada, which remained small because of the country's continued lack of interest in the field. To put this another way, when *Gone with the Wind* was a best-seller across the U.S. and Canada, Dudek and his fellow editors thought the term referred to the money he kept pouring into their publishing efforts. Voted the Least Poetic Canadian Poet from 1945 through 1982, Dudek lectured at McGill for more than three decades, since writing poetry, especially of the unemotional, intellectual kind, is no way to make a living.

SARA JEANNETTE DUNCAN

(1861 – 1922)

SARA Jeannette Duncan was born and bred in the town Wayne Gretzky made famous, and I don't mean Los Angeles, I mean Brantford, Ontario. Unfortunately Ms. Duncan couldn't play hockey worth a damn, so she had to depend on her writing for fame, if not fortune. She taught grade school for a while, then worked out a deal with several Canadian newspapers of the time: if they paid her, she would write a series of letters from various spots on the globe. It worked. She got out of Brantford, and Canada had one less writer clogging its streets. It was a no-lose agreement.

Duncan wrote for the Toronto *Globe* as a journalist; it was her good fortune as a woman that the paper wasn't *Male* yet. She also penned articles for the Montreal *Star*, but for that journal she wrote under a male pseudonym. It had worked for George Eliot, had it not?

More important to her career and our respect for her, since the paper was American, she also wrote for the *Washington Post*. Now you'll read this entry more carefully, yes?

She was even the parliamentary writer in Ottawa for the Montreal paper, in 1888, back when Montreal still gave a damn about what was going on in the nation's capital. Then in 1880, Duncan began to travel on the newly finished CPR on the start of a round-the-world tour, with another female journalist in tow. Once again, the well-travelled, and broadened, Sara Jeannette Duncan sent back articles to several newspapers across Canada (and the United States, don't forget). Her first book, published in 1890, *A Social Departure: How Orthodocia and I Went Round the World by Ourselves*, grew out of this journey. Jules Verne's *Around the World in Eighty Days* sold better.

Duncan then wrote with a frenzy and speed not to be seen in a Brantford native until the birth of The Great One, nearly three-quarters of a century later. This was in spite of the fact that she always needed assists and rarely fulfilled her goals.

While in India, Duncan met and married a museum curator when she was almost thirty. This led to her spending most of her remaining three decades of life in Calcutta.

However, she did head off to England and Canada for long visits on a regular basis. In point of fact, she amassed over 11.4 million miles on her frequent-traveller cards, but mostly on boats and trains, which was pretty impressive in the late nineteenth and early twentieth century.

Many of Duncan's two-dozen-plus books were actually published under her married name, Mrs. Everard Cotes, a fact that has appalled many a modern feminist Can Lit scholar. One novel, *The Imperialist*, published in 1904, is mostly set in Ontario. This salient fact did not help sales one iota; indeed, it probably hurt them. Luckily her other novels have India, America and Britain as their settings, which helped their sales quite a bit.

Duncan died in 1922 in England, which is fitting; like most Canadian writers before the modern era, she was never appreciated as much at home as abroad. And a broad she was, something that didn't help book sales much, either. And while she drifted quite far from her native Brantford, so did Wayne, and that didn't hurt *him* any, did it?

MARIAN ENGEL

(1933 – 1985)

A politically active author (on behalf of her fellow writers), and first chairman/woman/person of the Writers' Union, Marian Engel published some one dozen works of impressive fiction in her too short life. Toronto-born, small-town-raised, she wrote some highly creative and very funny books, including *The Honeyman Festival* (1970), *The Glassy Sea* (1978) and *Lunatic Villas* (1981), the latter initially popular in Ottawa, where many citizens assumed it was about the

Senate buildings. Engel's most shocking book, and not merely because it won the Governor General's Award (in 1976), was *Bear*, a book that gave a whole new meaning to the revered animal and nature stories category of Canadian literature.

TIMOTHY FINDLEY

(1930 –)

BORN in Toronto and educated around Ontario, "Tiff" Findley was first seen on Canadian and world stages instead of pages. In 1953, after having acted with the Earle Grey Shakespeare Company in Toronto, Findley joined the very first season of the Stratford Festival with such other performers as Don Harron, Douglas Campbell, Alec Guinness and William Shatner, and who ever hears about any of *them* nowadays? It was there, in a tiny Ontario town about a ninety-minute drive from Toronto, that he was almost adopted by Guinness, who sent him off to London to pursue an acting career. It was an actor's dream, but he was ultimately destined to become a far better writer, so some time was wasted in all that.

Findley performed for several years in the Mother Country, meeting with Thornton Wilder, acting in his play *The Matchmaker* in both London and New York and having that fine author criticize and encourage his writing. After working with Guinness and Wilder, one would think that Findley had had the ultimate good fortune in his friends, but don't forget how far another Canadian got with just a few months' acquaintance with Hemingway and Fitzgerald (see **Callaghan, Morley**).

In New York, and later in Hollywood, Findley continued

to write, while acting on the side. Or was it act, with writing on the side? With these multitalented Canadians, it's hard to know.

By 1962, Findley was writing for both radio and television and had begun to pen *The Last of the Crazy People*, which was published just in time for Canada's centennial year. Of course, since the play is about an eleven-year-old boy in a southern Ontario community, who, crushed by an oppressive upbringing and a family home of spiritual worthlessness and enervation, kills off his family members one by one, the book was less welcomed than a number of centennial hockey arenas of the same period.

By 1969, Findley had published *The Butterfly Plague*, which took place in Hollywood, unlike Findley's career. In the book another family is destroyed, this time by an inherited disease, although it is in fact the novel that is destroyed, by enough metaphors and symbols to keep Northrop Frye higher than a kite for a decade.

Timothy Findley's masterpiece is *The Wars* (1977), in which he recreates the life of a young Canadian named Robert Ross, using a narrator to bring together photographs, letters, news clippings and interviews. The book is so extraordinarily brilliant and so much better than *The Red Badge of Courage*, *All Quiet on the Western Front* and *The Naked and the Dead* that it is utterly impossible to make fun of, even though the book you are reading is one of satire and parody. Yet, despite its magnificence, *The Wars* won a Governor General's Award for fiction, is taught in many hundreds of Canadian high schools and has been translated into about a dozen languages. There's hope for this world yet.

Other books that have flowed from the prolific pen of Findley include *Famous Last Words* (1981), which has such utterly unbelievable, absurd characters — "the Duke of

Windsor," "the Duchess of Windsor," "Ezra Pound," "von Ribbentrop" and "Charles Lindbergh" — that only a novelist could have invented them; and *Not Wanted on the Voyage*, a retelling of the Noah story that is somehow much too watered down. Like most of his finest works, each of these books is daring, creative, intriguing, depressing, yet somehow still gay.

DAVID FRENCH

(1939 –)

BORN in Coley's Point, Newfoundland, a hotbed of fishing and jokes, David French moved to Toronto when he was six, a much earlier age than most natives of that province leave. He went with his parents, however, showing a lack of ingenuity and daring, something that would be echoed throughout most of his very traditional plays.

After studying acting, he performed on numerous CBC-TV dramas in the early 1960s, making nearly as much money and gaining almost as much fame as he would have, had he remained in Coley's Point, Newfoundland. Then, in 1962, the CBC bought his first play, *Behold the Dark River*, and more than a half-dozen more over that decade. But even the handful of people and fish left in Coley's Point didn't watch.

Finally French recognized that he was sitting on a goldmine of experiences upon which he had never drawn: the excitement of a teenage brother who got married too early; a father who had a penchant for getting drunk; an over-understanding mother; his own desire to get the hell away from a too early married brother, a too often drunk father, an overunderstanding mother. He called it *Leaving Home*, and after its opening at Toronto's important Tarragon Theatre in May 1972, it immediately became a staple of Canadian drama. Of course, hamburger is a staple of the Canadian diet, but that doesn't make it steak.

Looking back the nearly two decades since *Leaving Home* moved Toronto's critics to near ecstasy — it used to take a risqué foreign movie to achieve that, but this was the 1970s — it is quite understandable why such a decent, old-fashioned play could have such a profound effect. It showed Newfoundland families in precisely the light the rest of Canada wanted to see them in: marrying too young, getting drunk too often, being too understanding and leaving home too late in life.

Recognizing a good thing when he saw it — namely financial success: his first hit has had more than six dozen productions since its debut — French went on to write a second play with exactly the same characters, entitled *Of the Fields, Lately*, in 1973, which was essentially About the Same Thing, Boringly. The now wildly successful playwright — *Fields* has had nearly four dozen productions so far — went on to rewrite Chekhov, but Chekhov had done it much, much better.

In between a series of disappointing plays, French did have one major hit, *Jitters*, which was actually *not* about his Newfoundland family, and audiences were so relieved that they went wild with enthusiasm. It ran for four months in Toronto and was given productions in nearly every regional theatre across Canada, since the entire country was ecstatic to see an actual comedy by the usually dour French, as well as not to see another play about his family. An American production closed prematurely in Philadelphia before reaching Broadway, showing that Americans weren't as tired of the Mercer family as Canadians were, and therefore weren't bright enough to see what all the excitement was about.

Since then French has inflicted one more play about his family upon the public: *Salt-Water Moon*, in which he looks back to Newfoundland in the 1920s, when his mother and father were dating and planning marriage. During many of the performances, members of the audience would leap up and scream "DON'T DO IT!" and "IT'LL NEVER LAST, AND IT'S NIGH ON IMPOSSIBLE TO GET A DIVORCE IN NEWFOUNDLAND!" and "MAKE SURE YOU USE BIRTH CONTROL, NO MATTER WHAT THE CHURCH TELLS YOU!" Alas, the couple did get married and did have two sons, and you already know the results from the first two plays of the trilogy: a married too young son, a drunk too often father, a too understanding mother and a son who leaves home too late.

Recently David French promised that he might go back to his family's story again for at least two additional plays, maybe more. Petitions sprang up right across Canada, from Victoria, B.C., all the way to Coley's Point, Newfoundland, begging French not to follow through on his dread resolve.

FROM *LEAVING HOME*

MARY
I haven't even boiled up the salt cod for dinner, and already one son has knocked up his girlfriend and has to get married, and the other son graduates from high school, just like a goddam mainlander. What's this world coming to?

BEN
Oh, Mum! Calm down! I'll help you distill the

skreech and set the table. (*Looks around*) So, has Dad been carried back drunk from the pub yet?

MARY
Don't you talk fresh to me, young man! Just because you've just become the first kid to graduate high school in all of Newfoundland in over 250 years is no reason to gloat and feel all superior. Look at your kid brother! Billy's already gotten Kathy pregnant and has a whole life of poverty and despair ahead of him. But *you*? You think you're some kind of big shot.

BILL
Oh, take it easy, Mum. Ben just doesn't have his act together yet, that's all. He'll end up a drunk on pogey, too — don't you worry your head about it. (*Changes subject*) Hey, Ben — did you hear the latest mainlander joke? (*Pause*) How many Montrealers does it take to change a light bulb?

BEN
I heard it already. You know I'm a high school graduate, don't you? We studied all those in Grade Twelve.

MARY (*Keeping the peace*)
Ignore Ben, Bill. How many Montrealers? Tell me, Billy! I can't wait to hear!

BILL
None! They just sit around in the dark until a

Newf moves to town and does the hard work for them!

MARY (*Breaking into hysterical laughter*)
Oh, God, that's a *good* one! (*Slapping her side, breaking a hidden bottle of skreech*) You're a great one, Bill! No wonder you got Kathy to put out for you! (*Pauses*) Hey, do you think her mother will be sober enough to come to the wedding?

BEN (*Hurt by his mother's favouritism*)
The joke's not that funny, Mum. And anyway, Bill told it wrong. It's about Winnipeggers, and they need five Newfoundlanders, since three of them are too drunk to turn the light bulb and the other one keeps turning the ladder the wrong way.

BILL (*Scratching his head*)
God, you're right, Ben. You're always right. I'll never forgive myself for dropping out of Mainlander Jokes 309 in Grade Twelve! You're the greatest, Ben. (*Looks at sundial on his arm*) Hey, look! It's getting late. I've got to pick up my tux for my shotgun wedding and get really pissed before tonight so I can't perform on my wedding night, which is okay, 'cause Kathy's preggers already.

MARY (*Still laughing at joke*)
You see, Ben? Look at your brother! He's already got his priorities right, and he's a full year younger than you! He's a family man, he's a drunk and he has no future ahead of him. When are you going to figure out what to do with *your* life?

BEN (*Chagrined, but not sure of the meaning of the word chagrined*)
I don't know, Mum. I guess I just don't like the taste of rum that much, and I hate catching fish, so I really don't know *what* I'm going to do with my life. I sure wish I could hold my liquor like Dad, though. He doesn't collapse until after at least a dozen drinks.

MARY (*Chuckling*)
Well, let's hope we keep him down to less than a dozen before the wedding tonight! I hate when he fights with the priest. Just 'cause Father O'Reilly has that thing for altar boys is no reason for him to get so angry. I had to remind your dad last night that at least little boys don't get pregnant and don't need no abortions, which is against divine law. So what's the harm?

BEN (*Sensing her unease*)
You're angry at me, Mum. What is it this time?

MARY
Of course I'm angry, Ben. For one thing, you never get drunk with your dad and me anymore. For another, I sense that you are *ashamed* of your dad, which is why you didn't invite him to your high school graduation last night.

BEN
Oh, Mum, *that's* not it! I just couldn't drag him out of the bar in time to make the ceremony. You know I don't mind him always being drunk, but I was concerned that he'd throw up all over the other

grads' parents, like he did at all those Boy Scout meetings, and it gets the other people really upset.

MARY (*Hurt*)
I *knew* it! I *knew* it! You're *ashamed* of your dear father, just because he's a violent drunk! Name one other kid in your school who doesn't have a violent drunk as a father, and they sure as hell invite their fathers to their own high school graduations! You're ashamed of him, aren't you?

BEN
But Mum, you know that all the other dads carry puke-bags when they go to major public events, and Dad refuses to carry one and use it!

MARY
I'm surprised at you, Benjamin Mercer! Your father thinks that puke-bags are beneath him. He dropped out of school in kindergarten and was forced to go to work as a cod-tongue-cutter-outer, and he made a vow before the Holy Trinity that he would never lower himself to carrying and using a puke-bag. He felt that it was beneath him to act like a mainlander.

BEN
Mum, I don't want to talk about Dad any more. I've got something important to tell you. (*Pauses*) Something really important.

MARY (*Excited*)
You got a girl pregnant?

BEN (*Embarrassed*)
No, Mum. It's not that.

MARY (*Horrified*)
You're not going to tell me that you used a contraceptive, are you?

BEN (*Horrified*)
No, Mum. I'd never do a thing like that.

MARY (*Hopeful again*)
You've decided to become a drunk, just like your dad?

BEN (*Mortified*)
No, Mum. I'm sorry, but I just don't like the taste.

MARY (*Hopeful again*)
You're becoming a fisherman so you can work six weeks a year and spend the other forty weeks on welfare?

BEN (*More and more upset*)
No, Mum. It's not as good as that, I'm afraid. And anyway, there are forty-nine weeks in a year, not forty-four.

MARY (*Terror building up*)
What *is* it, then?

BEN (*Barely audible*)
Mum, I want to move out, go to Toronto and become a successful playwright, writing about this tedious family!

MARY (*She hears him, alas*)
Did you say that you plan to move out, go to Toronto and become a successful playwright writing about us?

BEN
Yeah, Mum. That's exactly what I said. Clearly, five decades of heavy drink hasn't hurt your hearing any.

MARY (*Purposefully*)
Where's the gun? I've got to find the gun. No son of mine is moving to Toronto. I'll *kill* him first. (*She spins around and shakes her finger at her son*) You just wait till your father gets carried home. If he's not too drunk, he'll blow your brains out.

BILL (*Rushing in*)
Hey, Ben! Mum! I just heard a great one from my knocked-up girlfriend just before she passed out from too much to drink. How can you tell which mainlander is the groom at a wedding?

BEN (*Bored*)
I've *heard* it before, Bill. I'm a high school graduate, remember? (*To MARY*) Mum, I'm going out to the pub to try to get drunk. The thought of my own mother wanting to kill me has turned me to drink.

MARY (*Tears in eyes; wiping her hands, wet from the home still, on her tattered dress, which she sewed herself*)
Oh, God! My oldest son following in his father's footsteps at last! Maybe he'll even become a fisherman . . . (*Her eyes stare into the future with*

hope) . . . or a village idiot . . . or an anthologizer of mainlander jokes . . . or even open a pub . . . or get a girlfriend preggers. . . . The sky's the limit now — the sky's the limit. (*She weeps for joy as her husband, Jacob, is carried in*)

NORTHROP FRYE

(1912 – but he'll live forever)

HE is the greatest literary mind in Canada, the greatest literary critic in Canada and the greatest world literature scholar in the world, which is like saying that Wayne Gretzky is a decent hockey player. Born in Sherbrooke, Quebec, and raised in Moncton, New Brunswick, Frye became one of the world's fastest typists. This would have led him nowhere, except for the fact that he eventually began to write the stuff he was typing. And Frye looked down upon what he had writteneth, and it was very good.

Frye studied at the University of Toronto — where he sure could have taught his professors a thing or three, and probably did — before being ordained as a United Church minister and even serving briefly as a preacher on the prairies. To say that his parish understood even a fraction

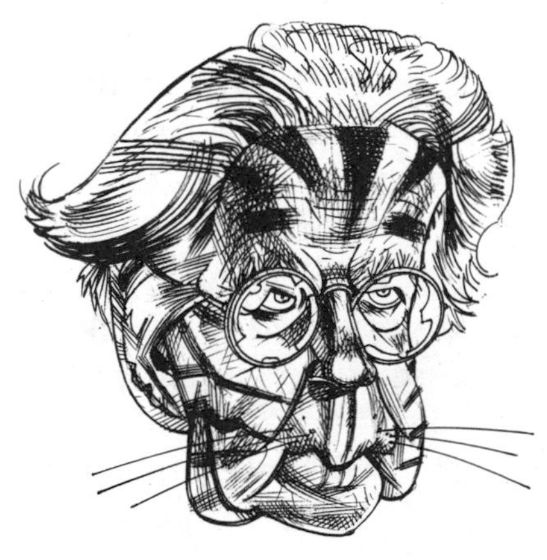

of what the hell and heaven Frye was talking about would be a statement of extraordinary generosity. He soon realized that he belonged in academia, but since Oxford, Cambridge, the Sorbonne and Everywhere Else weren't worthy of him, he settled for his alma mater, which he soon turned into a *grandmère* almost singlehandedly. No, make that singlehandedly.

Over the past half century, Frye has not only given the University of Toronto a reputation it had never before achieved, he has proceeded to create several masterpieces of world-class scholarship. In *Fearful Symmetry* (1947) he explained William Blake to everyone who hadn't understood the great British poet and artist before, which included every other Blake scholar before Frye. In *Anatomy of Criticism* (1957) he explained how myth and archetype worked in literature to everyone who hadn't understood it before, which included every other scholar of literature before Frye. In *The Bush Garden* (1971) he explained why Canadian literature is bush to everyone who is bright enough to listen (we won't discuss numbers here). In *The Great Code* (1982) he explained the patterns of the Old and New Testaments to all those willing to find them, and in this he was particularly fortunate: if he had done the same to the Koran, he could well have ended up in hiding like certain lapsed Muslim authors we know. And much, much more, including years of profound musings in the *University of Toronto Quarterly* (which he improved by halves in every issue) and his inspired Conclusion to the *Literary History of Canada* in 1965.

In brief, Frye is so magnificently intelligent and his writings so deeply thoughtful and original, the best I could do was to paraphrase some of his ideas from two of his key books, to try to give you a sense of his magnificent, thoughtful, original intelligence. It wasn't easy.

A FEW CONCEPTS FROM *ANATOMY OF CRITICISM*

COMEDY MAKES YOU LAUGH; tragedy makes you cry. Of course, when you watch situation comedies on CBC-TV, they tend to be tragic, which is a real problem. Comedies end in a marriage; tragedies end in a death. This has changed over the years, however, since marriages are no longer funny and usually end up tragically, which is a further problem.

Look at *Oedipus Rex*, for example. It is, inarguably, the perfect tragedy: a great man falls from power and grace because he killed his own father and married his own mother (which, according to Sigmund Freud, writing somewhat later, is the whole idea). Now, to kill your father and marry your mother is a tragedy. But if someone were to say to Oedipus, "Come on! You're not going to marry Jocasta, of all people! She's old enough to be your mother!" then we have a comedy, since it would end in a marriage and not in a death. Of course, Oedipus doesn't end in a death, but he does put his eyes out, which is the worst possible way to increase literacy, to which I have dedicated my life.

In a comedy, old people tend to stop young people from getting married. In a tragedy, old people tend to kill themselves and/or young people, which really isn't so tragic, when you consider some of the young people I've had in my courses at the U. of T. For me to have killed them would have been an act of mercy. And to think that many of them ended up in teaching yet. You can see why I've had my work cut out for me.

Satire, however, implies correction. In other words, the writer wishes society would change. This is why most politicians are ideal subjects for satire, especially Canadian politicians, because if anyone could use some change, it would be they. Or them. I can never get that one straight.

Then there's the romance, which we don't like to talk about in Canada, since we are too busy thawing out to do much of anything on the subject. Now, if *you* can find anything romantic about this country, let me know.

I hope you have this straight: comedy, tragedy, satire and romance. And then there's Canadian literature, which is comic in its attempts to be tragic and satiric in its attempts to be romantic. You can just *imagine* what greater heights I might have reached in my career if I had been born in London, England, instead of Sherbrooke, Quebec. The mind boggles.

A Smattering of *The Great Code*

THE BIBLE IS A COLLECTION of patterns, often intricate, occasionally subtle and all of them far too profound for simple folk such as you to have figured out before I deigned to write this book. The first book of the Old Testament is Genesis, as you know, but how many of you realize that "Gene" and "Sis" are the real names of the first couple in the Bible and not Adam and Eve, as was previously thought? Or that the first man mentioned in the Bible was, in fact, a fellow named Chap I?

But it is the patterns in the Bible that I am struck by, and that you had better be struck by, too, or you'll be struck down, especially if you're taking my Principles of Literary Symbolism course and actually expect to pass. For instance, there is a flood in the Old Testament, John the Baptist uses water to christen people in the New Testament and the toilets all back up in Nazareth, if I recall correctly.

Then there's Abraham's near sacrifice of his son Isaac, (leading to the still common expression "we've all got to make sacrifices," used most frequently by Canadian finance ministers) and God's sacrifice of His Only Begotten Son in the New Testament, which only goes to prove that God tends to follow through far better than men ever do.

And how about the twelve sons of Jacob, and the twelve apostles of Jesus, huh? Or the forty years in the desert of the Children of Israel (Joshua 5:6), the flood lasting forty days (Genesis 7:17), Moses spending forty days and nights on Mount Sinai (Exodus 34:28), Elijah fasting forty days (I Kings 19:8) and the forty days spent in the desert by Jesus in the New Testament? Or the terrible struggles between Cain and Abel, Isaac and Ishmael, Jacob and Esau and, much, much later, between me and Marshall McLuhan over becoming the most famous person ever to teach at the University of Toronto? Of course, Marshall and I weren't brothers, that's for sure. I'll tell you, there are patterns in the Bible and in life that you've never even dreamed of — did I mention the dreams of Jacob and Joseph and all the dreams in the New Testament? — which is why the Good Lord put me on the Earth, even if He for some reason or other chose to place me in Canada, which is a lot like Egypt in both the Old and the New Testaments by the way, except the weather was always much better in Egypt. But both are desert countries in their own way, as we all know, with Egypt being full of sand and Canada being full of pseudointellectuals and thus a scholarly desert, until I was created when the Lord gathered together dust from all over the world, blew His Holy Spirit into it and . . .

ROBERT FULFORD

(1932 –   )

A lucky man.

MAVIS GALLANT

(1922 –)

BORN IN MONTREAL, which is all that's really important, Mavis Gallant spent her youth in nearly twenty different schools in Canada and the United States, suggesting she could never find one place she really liked. She ended up being far more definite in her choice of country to live in, however, and it wasn't Canada.

Eventually Gallant began to write for the Montreal *Standard*, then worked a short while for the National Film Board, before heading off to Europe in 1950 and settling in Paris for most of the following four decades. Next to Alice Munro, she is the only Canadian author whose work appears regularly in the *New Yorker* — some 100 stories since 1951 — which drives most other North American writers into fits of insane jealousy.

Although Gallant has written some novels (*Green Water, Green Sky* in 1959; *A Fairly Good Time* in 1970) and the occasional extraordinary work of nonfiction, such as her journalistic coverage of the 1968 "student uprisings" in Paris (also first published in the *New Yorker*), she is most admired for her quite remarkable, haunting, lucid yet

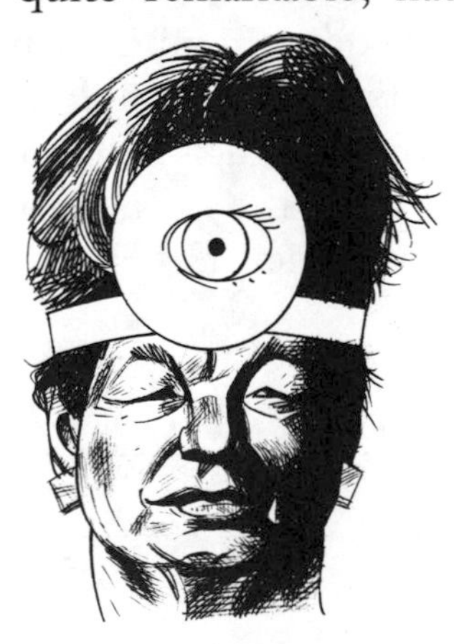

complex short story collections, including *The Other Paris* (1956), *My Heart Is Broken* (1964), *An Unmarried Man's Summer* (1964), *The Pegnitz Junction* (1973), *From the Fifteenth District* (1979) and *Home Truths* (1981), which won a Governor General's Award, just maybe because it is a collection of stories that are located in Canada, even if their author is not.

Interestingly, although Gallant had published many dozens of superb short stories in many magazines and had quite a few well-received books in hardcover by the mid-sixties, the first edition (1965) of the important *Literary History of Canada* did not even list them. It appears that no matter how much Canadian writers complain that they are ignored in their own land, when they move to another continent the chances of being ignored increase even further. Imagine if Gallant weren't one of the world's greatest writers of short stories; she wouldn't even have made this book.

But those are the dangers of leaving Montreal, moving to Paris and writing oodles of glorious short stories. All you end up with is world fame, if not necessarily Canadian fame. As the old cliché goes, she might have "made profits without honour in another land."

HUGH GARNER

(1913 – 1979)

BORN in Yorkshire, England, Hugh Garner was soon thrown into the pudding of Cabbagetown in Toronto, a fascinating little community of tiny, run-down gingerbread houses that today, barely a decade after his death, smart people white-paint and sell for $450,000 apiece. Garner once labelled the area "a sociological phenomenon, the largest Anglo-Saxon slum in North America," never knowing it would someday be too expensive for anyone to live in except expatriates from Hong Kong. Wealthy expatriates.

After Garner's father deserted his family, little Hugh did the same, heading west to cut wheat, work in relief camps and live the good life in R. B. Bennett's Canada of the thirties. As luck would have it, war came to save the economy, if not Japanese Canadians, so Garner went off to fight for the Loyalists in the Spanish Civil War, then for the Allies in the Canadian Navy.

Back in Canada, Garner began to write for a living, years before the Canada Council ensured that you don't have to be talented. *Storm Below* (1949) was about his wartime naval experiences, in which he contemplated his own. *Cabbagetown* followed in 1950, a depiction of working-class life in the depressing Depression Toronto.

Then came *The Silence on the Shore* (1962), *A Nice Place to Come From* (1970) and a series of police novels, including *Death in Don Mills* (1975), which isn't such a bad idea, when you think about it.

Garner spent his life and work celebrating the "little people" of Canadian society who had always been ignored in this country's literature: the migrant labourers, the Indians, the factory workers, the down-and-outers — you know, the sort of losers who can't afford a nice little $450,000 bungalow in Cabbagetown.

GRATIEN GÉLINAS

(1909–)

GREAT entertainer to French Canada between 1938 and 1946 with his famous *Fridolinons* stage revues and author of several interesting plays, he is best known and remembered for proving to the world that *Tit-Coq* are not dirty words.

Graeme Gibson

(1934 –   )

INTERESTING author of a handful of books, who lives with another interesting author who is quite a handful.

John Gray

(1946 –   )

ONE of Canada's most familiar playwrights, since he tends to insist on performing in his own shows and has recently been appearing on "The Journal" nearly as often as Barbara Frum, John Gray was born in Ottawa. Fortunately for him he was taken to Truro, Nova Scotia, where he could have a normal childhood among living people.

Gray is one of three brothers, all of whom became professional musicians. Yet John Gray never starved to death. Why is this? critics ask. For one thing, he played in a rock and roll band while attending Mount Allison University. For another, he got out of the Maritimes while the getting was good, and headed off to Vancouver, where the theatre wasn't.

Soon a fixture of the West, Gray could honestly brag he had been heard of from coast to coast. He studied acting and directing at the University of British Columbia, helping to found the Tamahnous Theatre. It wasn't lost until he directed some eight plays for them over the following few years.

From the very start — well, not from the *very* start, since he was born in Ottawa — John Gray dedicated himself to creating popular culture in a country where culture isn't popular. Fortunately popular is, so even though his writing isn't particularly cultured, it is popular, if you get what I mean.

Gray's first play was *18 Wheels* (1977), about the real Canada no one had ever dramatized: the all-night truckers and truckstop waitresses who make this country tick. (The people who make the country tock remain in Ottawa, busy making the lives of those who make this country tick all the more difficult. But Gray wouldn't write about the tockers until he became a regular on CBC-TV, which has ruined the talent of greater talents than he.)

Like all his plays, *18 Wheels* is filled with music, funny lyrics, love for the ordinary man and woman, and simple sets — just like Shakespeare, until the Stratford Festival killed the music, improved the lyrics, changed it to love between men and men and made the sets so cluttered with furniture audiences felt they were visiting an antique shop.

Gray's other works include *Rock and Roll* (1981), a sweet, harmless little musical about a group of small-town Canadian musicians who look back at their coming of age and realize they never have reached their coming of age, and here they are in their late thirties already, and *Don Messer's Jubilee*, a sweet, harmless little musical about a group of small-town Canadian musicians who look back on a country that never has come of age musically, and here it is in its second century already. He has also written several children's plays, including *Bongo from the Congo* and *Balthazar and the Mojo Star*, which have the same complexity and profundity as his plays for adults.

His greatest success has been *Billy Bishop Goes to War* (1978). It toured Canada for sixteen months, then finally was discovered by American theatrical giant Mike Nichols in 1980, who helped it to reach Washington and New York, where it was liked even more. This inevitably led to the Governor General's Award for drama in 1982, since if the Americans liked it, it must be good.

It was.

GREY OWL

(1888 – 1938)

WE HATE to break it to you, but he really was a honkie (see **Belaney, Archie**).

FREDERICK PHILIP GROVE

(1879 – 1948)

GROVE was not the first (nor will he be the last) Canadian writer who would write a better life than he had lived. Actually, his life, as we read in his autobiography, *In Search of Myself* (1946), was a most romantic one. He was born in Russia while his wealthy parents were visiting that country; his father was the son of an Englishman who had owned a large castle in Sweden, where Grove lived until he was in his early teens. After attending school in Berlin and at the Sorbonne, where he studied archaeology, he travelled around the world, before ending up in Haskett, Manitoba, which certainly seems a letdown, no matter how you look at it.

A truly romantic life, indeed, since it was all lies. Grove was actually born Greve in Prussia and raised by parents in

Hamburg. He eventually stole money from a childhood chum and spent a year in prison for fraud. After that, even a teaching job in rural Manitoba must have looked good.

Once he reached Manitoba, Greve/Grove's career took off, at least in terms of output. His first book written in English (or so the critics claim) was *Over Prairie Trails* (1922). It sounds like a cowboy novel, except the only people who die are the readers, many of whom are bored to death. Then came *Settlers of the Marsh* (1925), begun in German but reportedly completed in English. It was extremely controversial, since it had graphic sex scenes. In any other country this would have meant runaway sales. In Canada, it offended the public, who wouldn't buy it, and the libraries, who refused to carry it. This has led many sociologists to wonder how Canadians even managed to have children during these years, and how they knew what to put where.

Other nonbest-sellers followed, including *A Search for America* (even in 1927, having "Canada" in a book title was the kiss of death); *The Master of the Mill* (1944); and his greatest work of fiction, his autobiography, *In Search of Myself*. (Clearly the search failed.) Throughout all these books, Grove always managed to drive his readers batty with endless detail, wooden and stilted language and plots that were never as exciting as his life story. It is not by chance that Grove lived for a decade in Poverty, a small farming community just outside of Simcoe, Ontario, where only the cattle got fed. He suffered a stroke in 1944, after which he was supported by his fellow writers (honour among thieves), and died in 1948, although no one can really know for sure. After all, he had faked a suicide when he snuck out of Europe in 1909, so maybe he had done it again. If he *is* still alive, he is over 110 years old and, God forbid, still writing.

THE PLOT OF *THE MASTER OF THE MILL*

SAM CLARK IS THE MASTER of the mill, if nothing else. The book takes place in the mind of this very old man, which may recall **Margaret Laurence's** *The Stone Angel*, except the latter is really interesting. The story opens with the elderly Sam looking out at the giant mill, which may recall the opening of *The Mountain and the Valley*, except in Buckler's book, the author is kind enough to kill the protagonist off in the end. We don't even get that pleasure here, even though Sam is in his eighties. One only hopes some critic will beat the man to death.

The novel moves wildly back and forth between 1939 and 1882, and covers in the process all the great things that happened during Sam's life. For instance, we meet his father, Rudyard, who is driven by a longing for money and who dies of a sudden stroke, which might be a moral for us. Sam, on the other hand, only longs to use the mill to improve the quality of life for everyone, which makes us wonder why our Canadian politicians don't feel the same way. (Indeed, Grove actually ran unsuccessfully for the CCF in a provincial election in 1943, when he really should have run for cover.) Edmund Clark, Sam's son, outmanoeuvres his dad at a stockholders' meeting and manages to take over the mill — sort of like the Ballards, except that they could be fun, if tiresome. Edmund also hopes to improve the lot of future generations with his mill, but he tends to ignore the present generation and automates everything within sight. This throws everyone out of work, and Edmund gets shot by disgruntled workers, who tended to be the only kind around in those days. Sam now gets the mill back, and the reader is left wondering if the old bugger is ever going to kick the bucket, if not the mill. The younger reader is also left wondering if the damned book will be on the exam.

The novel has three female characters named Maud: Sam's wife, who loves culture more than the mill; Maud Doolittle, Sam's sympathetic secretary, who understands Sam's love for the mill more than the reader; and Maud Fanshawe, the wife of Edmund, and therefore Sam's daughter-in-law. This wondrously coincidental use of the same name has enraged critics and irritated the public, but Grove's inclusion of three women with the same first name helped Jack McClelland in his attempts to sell the book in his New Canadian Library series, with one of the publisher's greatest publicity stunts — *THREE!* THAT'S RIGHT! *THREE* MAUDS FOR THE PRICE OF *ONE!*"

The book has been justly compared to Joseph Conrad's *Lord Jim* in that the reader is forced to put all the pieces of the past together. Of course, Conrad was born and raised in Poland, and changed his name, but never denied either, and, unlike Grove, took the trouble to learn English.

THOMAS CHANDLER HALIBURTON

(1796 – 1865)

BORN in Windsor, Nova Scotia, Haliburton was the only child of Tory and Loyalist parents — the nineteenth-century equivalent of ethnic. He graduated from King's College in his home town in 1815, then began to practise law in Annapolis Royal, until he got it right.

Haliburton was elected to Nova Scotia's legislative assembly in 1826, and in 1829 he became a judge, lest not he be judged. Eventually he worked his way up to the Supreme Court of Nova Scotia, which left him lots of time to write.

Later in life, Haliburton began to spend more and more of his time in England, eventually settling there permanently in 1856. This limited his time spent on the bench in Nova Scotia, but he didn't seem to mind. He even managed to win a seat to the British House of Commons, yet was never accused of "dual loyalty" by his former neighbours back in Nova Scotia

The first writings of Haliburton were on the history and geography of Nova Scotia, subjects his future countrymen in England had been climbing the wall to read about. When these didn't sell too well, he created the eternal, infernal character of Sam Slick the Clockmaker, whose fictional experiences were published in Joseph Howe's famous newspaper, the *Nova Scotian*. Although these satirical little stories about an aggressive Yankee salesman weren't particularly dirty or violent, they were still hugely successful, making Haliburton a celebrated writer in both the United States and England, where it really counted. Canadians liked him, too.

Profoundly involved in Canadian political issues, Haliburton fought against Lord Durham's report and was a vigorous opponent of the Maritimes uniting with Upper and Lower Canada, feeling this would lead to annexation to the United States. In the late twentieth century, most Canadians wouldn't mind at all if parts of their country were annexed, since they could get electronic goods so much more cheaply then.

Most critics feel that Haliburton was one of the founders of North American humour for his remarkable use of regional dialects. (In other words, no one can get the gags anymore.) Had he recreated the dialects of blacks or Orientals, he would be labelled a racist, but since he mocks Nova Scotians and their own silly accents, no one really cares.

FROM *THE CLOCKMAKER*
(1836)

WHAT A PITY IT IS, Mr. Slick" (for that was his name, and a pretty funny one, you've got to admit) "that a man like yourself, who has had such a success in teaching all these dumb Canadians the value of *clocks*, has been unable to teach them the value of *time*."

"Hey, that's a good one!" Slick said in that patronizing way Yankees love to talk down to us Canadians. "Well, you see," he said, "we Americans actually think that time is important, that it's *money*. You Canadians can't even figure out what time it is in Newfoundland."

"Hey, that's a good one!" I told him in that disarming way we Canadians love to talk down to those stinking, crooked, rotten-through-and-through Yankee scumbags.

"A sight better than yur joke," Slick said. "But of course you lousy Canucks have no *idea* about time. All you do is drink, eat, sleep, drink, sleep and eat, and usually all at the same time, which is *dreck* for the digestive system. All you *schmucks* do is talk 'bout politics, when ev'ryone knows that Maritime politics don't count *bupkes* in your country. Or anywhere else, for that matter."

"Boy, you really *are* a savage one!" I said to him, thrilled that he could be so critical about Canada and knowing that if I put such honest, true feelings in my *own* character's mouth, I'd be hung in Effigy, which is a small town in the Annapolis Valley. "But how do you manage to sell *so* many clocks," I said, "to a people who lack both time and the money to pay for them?" I smiled inwardly at my own keen wit.

"Oh, h — ," Slick declared, in that witty, obscene manner that endears the Yankees so much to us Canadians. "It's *easy* to sell anything to the *schmendricks* up here. You *schlemiels* don't know your *tucheses* from a hole in the ground, with your *fersluggíner* politicians, your *farblonget* judges and your *schlemazzeldik* farmers. *Farshtay?*"

"Je *farshtay*," I said, at my bilingual best.

"It's all 'soft sawder and human natur'," he replied, laughing. "I just use 'soft sawder,' and can sell to any *grubber yung* in the Maritimes."

"Forgive me," I interrupted him. "But what does 'soft sawder' mean?"

"You don't understand English?" exploded the clock-maker in a rage. "No wonder you *goyim* will never get anywhere in this world. *Gai geharged.*"

I quickly purchased his last two dozen clocks for $40.00 each and headed off into the night, proud of my bargaining expertise — they must have cost him at least $6.50 to make — and vowing to learn the American language or die trying. Soft sawder, indeed.

CHARLES HEAVYSEGE

(1816 – 1876)

THIS great nineteenth-century playwright was born in England, a fact that continued to constitute a great literary advantage in Canada well into this century. (Do recall that performing the semicompetent plays of John Galsworthy, J.M. Barrie, Christopher Fry and Noel Coward was considered Canadian theatre right into the 1960s.)

Heavysege published his first verse drama, *The Revolt of Tartarus*, in 1855, in Montreal, anonymously. No one has ever blamed him. Since it consisted of six books of blank verse, no one will ever blame him in the future, either. Interestingly, he published an edition in England three years earlier with his name on it, which explains why he headed off to Canada in 1853.

His new home would be Montreal, where *hommes* were men, *dames* were broads and poets were ignored. And where, more than a century ago, it was still a great advantage to know English.

Once in this country, Heavysege became a kind of hewer of wood, doing carpentry work and making better cabinets than Pierre Trudeau ever would. Of course, unlike today's politicians, whether federal or provincial, the poet had something substantial to work with.

Throughout his life, Charles Heavysege was a quiet eccentric who chose to compose unstageable, dumb, pretentious, pseudo-Elizabethan dramas that were only 300 years late and utterly devoid of talent. But his plays gained great respect and even raves from a large number of American and British critics. His *Saul: A Drama in Three Parts*, inflicted on readers in 1857, was praised as "indubitably the best poem ever written out of Great Britain." Looking over the previous few dozen pages of this anthology, you can quickly gather just how damning with faint praise that statement is.

Being a true Canadian nationalist, Charles Heavysege wrote about themes that spoke intimately to his chosen countrymen: *Saul*, as noted above; *Jephthah's Daughter* (1868); and horribly numerous sonnets that are as unreadable as his plays, if possibly more stageable.

Was Charles Heavysege a great playwright? Is the Pope Protestant?

From *Saul*, Act XXII, Scene lviv

SAUL
Get thee gone. I do no longer need thou!

(*Exit* ATTENDANT,
pursued by boredom)

I swear by gum that he shall die! Why did
I spare him, when just now I had sworn so?
Why have I sworn his life should be so dear
To please that idiot, fair Jonathan?
I'll smash all oaths
If they shall stand between me and my mind.
Let Jonathan beware, or he'll regret
That he stood between David and my rage!

(*Exit, and enter*
MALZAH *in Mazda*)

MALZAH
For sure, now he'll kill David, and thus end
My slavery. But what hath this to do
With Canada, or any part of this huge land?

(*Exit, and enter*
DAVID *in fur, along*
with the QUEEN, *in*
Creeds)

QUEEN
Oh, you are a sight for sore eyes!
But now, alas, my speech is done, for
It is time to make my exit, no sooner
Hath I made my entrance, forsooth.

(*Exit, but not missed*)

SAUL
(*Entering, having thrown javelin that looks*

strangely like a hockey stick at DAVID, *who has escaped as before, guaranteeing at least another few acts*)

Dammit! Missed again!
How sharper than a serpent's tooth to
Have a lousy aim!
He came unto his doom — pissoff! — I've blown it!
But I shall hound him till he dogs his day!

(*Enter an* OFFICER *and* SOLDIERS)

Here you are at last!
Go, seize the paths to David's tent,
And kill him 'ere he says his morning prayers.

OFFICER
That's not niceth!

SAUL
Oh, shut upeth. This is not Canada,
But ancient Palestine, where people
Truly roughed it in the burning bush.

OFFICER
Okay, then. Sorry. I'll do the deed.

(*Exeunt* OFFICER *and* SOLDIERS, *the latter without a chance to get even one word in edgewiseth*)

SAUL
Now I've had it up to here (*Motioneth to neck*)
With this lad.
I have no room for pity, no room at th'inn,
With mixeth metaphors but mightily.
All kindness now is gone; my heart is cold,
But I will get the neck of that young whippersnapper yet.
How can I wait till morn for tidings brought?

MALZAH (*Entering as though he never left*)
Oh, dear, I bleweth it! I am ashamed.

SAUL
Not half as shamed as Heavysege should be!
To write a play that cannot e'er be staged
Till Burnham Wood come fifth toward Dunce, inane.

MALZAH
No wonder theatre lovers gnawed on bone
Until the coming hence of Nathan Cohen.

(*Exeunt, hopefully ne'er to return*)

ANNE HÉBERT

(1916 –   )

BORN in Ste-Cathérine-de-Fossambault, a town English wasn't heard in, even at the local Eaton's, Anne Hébert was sickly in her youth, making it necessary for her parents to educate her. As it happened, her father was a critic and a respected poet; in other parents' hands, she could have ended up sounding like a hockey player. Indeed, her father actually urged his lovely, talented daughter to write, something about which we warn other Canadian parents: *do not try this at home*. Her youth was spent in Quebec City, and by the 1950s, she got out when the getting was good, heading off to Paris, where she has remained off and on ever since (see also **Gallant, Mavis**; she's in the Parisian phone book).

Hébert had become a respected poet by the time she was in her mid-twenties, publishing many fine poems and having a number of her plays performed, but her greatest success came with her best-known novel, *Kamouraska* (1970), based on an actual murder committed in the previous century (see **Reaney, James**).

The work has two plots. The first begins in 1839, when a young woman named Elisabeth talks her American lover into killing her husband, who is a violent man and a big shot in Kamouraska. (So much for Free Trade.) The killer, Dr. Nelson, flees to the United States, which is typical of the Yankees. Elisabeth is arrested, put in prison and eventually released, finally marrying a man from Quebec City, since it's obvious that Americans can't be trusted. The second plot is set two decades later, when Elisabeth's hubby number two, Rolland, is dying, leaving our questionable heroine with a question: should she remain in Quebec City or go off to her former lover, who was a killer in bed, not to mention with hubby number one? Since the heroine is a Canadian woman, even if one with blood on her hands, you can probably guess her choice (see **Hémon, Louis**). Still, to live a life of horror, passion and guilt, and to be eventually played by Geneviève Bujold, is a fate that few Québécois women can even dream of. There is an example here for all Canadian housewives with nasty husbands.

LOUIS HÉMON

(1880 – 1913)

To this day Louis Hémon projects the ideal image of the Canadian novelist: he was born in France, studied at the Sorbonne, lived in England for eight years, then spent only two years in Canada, before being run over by a train at the age of thirty-three.

Hémon was actually born in Brest, France, which led to a lifelong fetish. Since his father was the inspector general of Public Education of France, young Louis knew he had better study hard or Daddy would do something cruel to him, such as sending him off to Canada. But, no. The lad did well in university, graduated from law school and served in the military — three things that in no way prepared him for a future writing career. Or avoiding an oncoming train, for that matter.

In 1903, Hémon was off to England in search of the other official language of Europe. For nearly a decade he served as a correspondent for a French sports magazine, winning a number of literary contests along the way. Clearly this was to be no ordinary Canadian writer.

During those same years, Hémon married a young woman named Lydia O'Kelly. The marriage provided him with the sort of background that would serve him in good stead in Canadian politics. Yet he chose to leave both his wife and an infant daughter when he headed off to his new home and native land in 1911. A man of insight and intelligence, he was clearly familiar with the fact that Canada was no place to raise a family.

But it was just as clearly okay to write a book about what he didn't know. Indeed, after spending less than eighteen months in Canada, he penned the definitive novel on French-Canadian society, *Maria Chapdelaine*, a work that helps explain why Québécois have always been wary of anyone but their own kind: they might carry pens, talk funny and think they know it all.

Which Louis Hémon obviously did, for his book became an instant classic, selling well around the world not long after it was first published, posthumously, in 1914. And although selling one's books posthumously is certainly no way to make a living, at least the royalties gave his bereft widow and fatherless child back in England something to remember him by.

Of course, critics today know full well that Hémon did *not* know it all, because he clearly didn't know enough to get out of the path of that train back in 1913.

It is obvious why *Maria Chapdelaine* was so eagerly welcomed in France, across Europe and most especially in English Canada when it was finally translated into that tongue. After all, it told readers what they wanted to know: that all Québécois are illiterate peasants, depressed, stunned and crushed by the church. And there are still some Canadians who wonder why the Separatists are popular.

A Brief Plot Outline of *Maria Chapdelaine*

MARIA IS A YOUNG WOMAN born to a restless farmer who is determined to cut down the forest and turn it into agricultural property, utterly unaware that the big bucks lie in having a farm that you tear up and turn into a highway. Both Samuel Chapdelaine and his long-suffering wife, Laura, continually move deeper and deeper into the forest, far from neighbours, the church and the cops, who presumably are after him.

The Chapdelaine homes are forever being threatened by the forest around them, something far more reminiscent of Atwood's *Survival* than of Disney's Chip 'n' Dale. But Maria has a number of suitors, all of whom offer to Take Her Away From All This, which really shouldn't have been too hard, except that where she was living was truly nowhere.

Demonstrating a profound understanding of the French-Canadian experience, the entire novel consists of Maria's never getting what she wants. In the first portion of the book, Maria falls in love with a man of the forest, symbolically named François Paradis. He is a logger, and logs several happy hours with her, vowing to come back from the logging camp as soon as possible and promising her his hand. It is clearly a less visible part of his body that she desires, however.

And so François leaves, taking Maria's heart with him, although *he* was hoping for a more visible part of *her*. He declares that he will marry her in the spring, which is what they all say.

Alas the spring runs dry, since on the way back to visit the woman of his dreams (although it's *his* name that means "paradise" — hers means "protective wool covering"), he dies of the cold, having forgotten to plug himself in when he went to sleep. Maria is devastated, but must still manage to survive another half-dozen chapters. Life was like that in the woods.

Fortunately those six chapters see two other suitors pledge their troths, which is the way sex was handled in the last century. Lorenzo Surprenant, surprisingly, comes and offers Maria a new life in the United States, once he gets his green card. There she'll live in a bustling town with lots of churches to crush her spirit whenever she's in the mood. It's everything her poor mother had dreamed of, but her mother (and the author) conspire to destroy it: Mama Chapdelaine dies, presumably of a chronic case of disappointment, and Maria quickly comes to realize that her *real* future lies in the despair, lousy weather and enriching tradition of her native province, good ol' illiterate, peasant, backwoods Quebec.

And so, Maria manages to continue the glorious tradition her mother had so patiently laid out for her: loneliness, depression and all the ice, snow and scenery she can eat. Understandably, Maria Chapdelaine agrees to marry Eutrope Gagnon, a man who clears land, just like her dear old dad, and who promises her *everything* her mother managed to achieve in her own nasty, brutish and short life. There are to be no "paradises" or "surprises" in Maria's life. This is after all Canada, where compromise reigns (when it's not snowing). But at least Maria ends up with a guy, which is why the book remains popular around the world to this day. Usually the heroine doesn't end up with anyone at all because most men are creeps (see **Atwood, Margaret**) or gay (see **Findlay, Timothy; Tremblay, Michel**) or already married (see **Almost Everyone Else**).

JOHN HERBERT

(1926 –)

BORN in, as well as bored by, Toronto, John Herbert Brundage wrote the Great Homosexual Play long before there were greats, homosexuals *or* plays in his native country. Based on an incident in his youth when he was beaten and robbed by a street gang, for which he was sent to a reformatory for six months (Canadian justice always has worked in strange ways — recall the treatment of Japanese Canadians and Donald Marshall), he turned the experience into his only successful theatrical piece, *Fortune and Men's Eyes*.

Since the play was actually good, no one would touch it except the late theatre critic Nathan Cohen, who sent it off to a New York producer. It opened off Broadway in 1967, and as of the end of the 1980s, it had been performed in more than 100 countries and translated into more than three dozen languages.

Naturally, its first professional production in Toronto did not occur until 1975, since things tend to move more slowly in Canada, what with the bad driving conditions and all. Then again, *Anne of Green Gables* was first published in Boston, so what we've got going here is a tradition.

Since the international (and only occasionally national) success of *Fortune*, Herbert has written several other works, which are neither great nor plays but which certainly continue to be homosexual. It's painful to peak when you're so young and not develop afterward. But, then, look at the career of Joe Clark. Clearly what we've got going here is another Canadian tradition.

FROM *FORTUNE AND MEN'S EYES*

A CANADIAN REFORMATORY; prep school for provincial politics.

ROCKY (*Screaming*)
Oh, shut up!

MONA
I haven't even *said* anything yet! The play just *began*, for chrissake!

ROCKY
I know, you flaming queen. I just felt like blurting that out to express to the audience my viciousness and inner hardness.

QUEENIE (*Sings*)
Oh, if I had the wings of an angel
And the tush of a wild kangaroo,
I'd hop over downtown Toronto
To drop down my kangaroo poo. . . .

GUARD (*Entering with* SMITTY)
Okay, you guys, cut out the vulgarities. This is Ontario in the late forties. Nothing open Sundays, bars that close at 9:30 and a self-righteousness you don't even have to be homosexual to resent. (*To* SMITTY) Here's your new home, Smitty. Keep it clean. This is Ontario in the late —

MONA
Oh, can it, ya dumb screw! Welcome, big boy! Whatcha do wrong?

SMITTY (*Breaking down in tears*)
I . . . I . . . I, uh, littered. I didn't mean to, I swear! The cigarette butt burned my hand, and I just couldn't —

ROCKY (*Leaping for* SMITTY'S *throat*)
You dirty sonovabitch! I'll *kill* you for that!

QUEENIE (*Anxious for piece/peace*)
Now, now, girls! The kid *said* he didn't mean it! (QUEENIE *puts his arms around* SMITTY, *trying*

to comfort him, not to mention feeling his back, which is hot stuff for a Canadian play)

MONA (*Jealously*)
So, Rocky — are *you* so perfect? What got *you* in here?

ROCKY (*Falling back on bed, smoking*)
I'd rather not talk about it. (*Clearly upset*)

MONA (*Taunting him mercilessly*)
Come on, Rocky! What *did* you do to get yourself in the can?

ROCKY (*Breaking down in tears*)
I . . . I . . . I had this lemonade stand, which I opened . . . which I . . . opened —

QUEENIE (*Horrified*)
No! Nooooooo!

ROCKY (*Weeping bitterly*)
Which I opened . . . on a Sunday. . . .

MONA (*In a rage*)
On a Sunday? You opened a business on a *Sunday*? You dirty, filthy bastard, I could *kill* you for that! (*He throws himself on* ROCKY, *partly to fight with him, but also to feel his hard, steely chest*) Have you no respect for the Canadian family? (*He slaps* ROCKY) For the need to go to church? (*He slaps* ROCKY *again*) Christ, don't you realize that this is Ontario in the late 1940s?

ROCKY (*Trying to protect his face*)
Look! Lay off! Leave me alone! I swear on my mother's grave that I didn't open until Sunday *afternoon*, long after most Canadians had returned home from church! It was the afternoon that I opened up, I swear!

MONA (*Getting off him*)
All right, then. I believe you. And thanks for the physical contact. I needed that.

ROCKY (*Smiling shyly*)
Was it good for you?

MONA (*Winking*)
The best.

SMITTY (*Shaken by what's happened*)
What's going *on* here? This isn't the quiet, friendly, heterosexual world I had grown accustomed to at home!

ROCKY (*Sneering, snarking, snorkeling*)
Welcome to the hard, embittered world of a Canadian reformatory, Smitty. A place populated with litterers, with guys who open businesses on Sunday, and more. . . .

SMITTY (*Shocked beyond belief*)
I can't *believe* this. What is this world coming to?

GUARD (*Bursting in; hard; bitter*)
Worse than you or our audience can ever imagine, Smitty. There are men here who smoke cigarettes

without filters. (QUEENIE *gasps*) There are others who don't have life insurance. (MONA *faints*) There are even those who have had a drink in a Toronto bar without any food to go along with it to take an edge off any potential intoxication. (ROCKY *rushes to the toilet in the corner and throws up*)

SMITTY (*Rushing to the bars of the cell, trying to get out*)
Let me out of here! *Let me out!*

GUARD (*Maliciously*)
There are even guys in here who don't care if Portuguese, Maltese, Chinese, Greeks, Jews, Italians, Japanese, Pakistanis, even French Canadians actually move into this province! (*All the prisoners begin to scream; then they knock down the* GUARD, *grab his keys and make a run for it. The entire audience gets up and rushes out of the theatre, as well, in horror and panic. After all, this* is *Ontario in the late 1940s*)

JACK HODGINS

(1938–)

THE man who made the northern part of Vancouver Island famous, British Columbia-born and -educated Hodgins has made the readers of such books as *The Invention of the World* (1977), *The Resurrection of Joseph Bourne* (1980) and *The Barclay Family Theatre* (1981) laugh with pleasure and thrill to their daring plots and quirky characters. For this he was banished for a time to Ottawa to teach. Communist countries used to jail their better writers. Canada just ignores them. (See **many other men and women** in this book, make note of whether they have to teach to survive, and you'll understand.)

HUGH HOOD

(1928 –)

BORN in Toronto to a French-Canadian mother and a father who hailed from Nova Scotia, Hugh Hood should have been a politician, since he had the family background for it — in Canada, being Catholic has never been a deterrent to success. Instead he chose to write more books than his fellow citizens are capable of reading.

The key to Hood's youth is that he attended the Our Lady of Perpetual Writing Parish School in Toronto, where he first made the assumption that he should never put down his pen. Thus, he wrote part of a novel in 1954 called *The Beginning of Wisdom*, which was never completed; wrote another novel over the next few years entitled *God Rest You Merry*, which remains unpublished; and created another novel in 1959 called *Hungry Generations*, which was also never published. After this came a steady stream of very fine short stories, which *were* published, and an even steadier stream of very questionable novels, which were published but remain unread.

Armed with a Ph.D. from the University of Toronto, and therefore dangerous, he taught English for many years at the Université de Montréal, produced several novels in the 1960s and 1970s, then began, in 1975, a twenty-five-year project of creating (and yes, publishing) a series of twelve *(12)* interrelated novels under the title *The New Age*. The novels have been coming out inexorably, inevitably, indisputably, inconceivably, indefatigably and indecisively, as well as in hardcover, ever since, with the final books due to be finished in the year 2000, when a lot of religions will be looking forward to the End, as well. Of course, by that time, all diseases might be cured, Trudeau might be back in power in Ottawa (with Mackenzie King as his minister of Strangeness) and Winnipeg, thanks to the greenhouse effect, could have the climate of Barbados. Which will mean that lots of Canadians will have the time to read Hood's series. Until then, only debt can weaken Hugh's determination to pull the Hood over the eyes of his fellow Canadians.

JANET TURNER HOSPITAL

(1942 –)

BORN and raised in Australia, the young writer went from Down Under to Up Over, family settling in Kingston, Ontario, after various journeys to Los Angeles, Boston and India. She became a highly respected novelist with the publication of *Borderline* (1985), *Dislocations* (1986) and *Charades* (1989), but since in this country money is what it's all about, let us just note that Ms. Hospital won the $50,000 Seal First Novel Contest in 1982 with *The Ivory Swing*. Most Canadian novelists don't see $50,000 in their lifetimes unless they work in banks (see **Service, Robert W.**; **Souster, Raymond**; and **Berton, Pierre**, who never worked in a bank, but who laughs his way to one every few months when royalty payments come pouring in).

W. P. KINSELLA

(1935 –   )

BORN in Edmonton, Alberta, William Patrick Kinsella soon dedicated himself to doing for baseball what the Montreal Expos have never managed to do: give it beauty, talent, consistency and art. And even make bundles of money from that sport, as well, something else the Expos seem destined never to do.

Kinsella studied at the University of Victoria before going into business for nearly twenty years. Then he heard the call of the wild, which in fact was some drunken bums in the bleachers, and decided to go off and earn a Master of Fine Arts at the famous Writer's Workshop of the University of Iowa. He soon began to unleash a veritable flood of writing, primarily on baseball and Indians, two of North America's favourite pastimes, since both involve hitting, striking out, sliding home, rainouts, reservations, career-ending injuries, forgotten heroes and more.

Kinsella was writing stories about Indians (*Dance Me Outside* in 1977, *Scars* in 1978, *Born Indian* in 1981, *The Moccasin Telegraph* in 1983 and others) long before it was decreed that it was racist and offensive for a white man to do such a thing. Of course, Kinsella can't play baseball worth a damn, and no one has yet pointed out that it's wrong for a white man to write about such a black-and-Hispanic-dominated sport.

Kinsella has penned numerous short stories about baseball, and novels, as well, the most famous being *Shoeless Joe*, a lovely, magical and poetical story about an Iowa farmer who is called by a strange voice to build a baseball diamond in his cornfield so Shoeless Joe Jackson, cruelly disgraced in the 1919 fixing scandal, can return to play. The book was turned into a wildly successful movie, *Field of Dreams*, which may well have been the silliest movie ever made, except that every movie has not been made yet.

In the book, the reclusive American writer J. D. Salinger is kidnapped and taken to the farm of the narrator (wittily and subtly named "Ray Kinsella") to watch baseball played by lots of talented, but dead, men so that his pain will be healed. However, in the movie, due to threats of a lawsuit from Salinger, the character was changed to that of a black ex-hippie has-been overacting writer, which makes about as much sense as building a baseball diamond in a cornfield. Now that you've seen the movie, read the book. The movie is Iowa. The book is heaven.

WILLIAM KIRBY

(1817 – 1906)

A name known to, if not loved by, students of early Canadian fiction, if not literature, British-born Kirby was brought to the United States as a teenager, which meant that when he drifted up to Canada and eventually to Niagara-on-the-Lake a few years later, he became the definitive United Empire Loyalist. Although he wrote several books of poems and various narratives, his fame (?) rests upon *The Golden Dog* (1877). It became a best-seller and an Alternate Selection of the Unliterary Guilt Book Club.

A historical romance of eighteenth-century Quebec, *The Golden Dog* was impressively subtitled "a romance of the days of Louis XV in Quebec," a description containing more words than most Canadian teenagers read in a month in the late twentieth century. Le Gardeur de Repentigny, an army officer, loves the angelic Angélique, who is as sweet as Margaret Thatcher. Indeed, Angélique longs to make love to the powerful intendant of Lower Canada, François Bigot, as a kind of pioneer groupie. Meanwhile, Le Gardeur has a sister, Amélie, who also has hot blood, but flowing through cleaner veins. She's got a crush on Pierre Philibert, whose father runs the store with the same name as the book's title. There is murder, passion, terror, revenge, cries, greed, treachery, screams, villainy, ambition and lust in this novel of more than 600 pages. And all that happens on the first page alone — kind of like today's *Hansard.*

A. M. KLEIN

(1909 – 1972)

EVEN though his name began with two initials, just like E. J. Pratt, A. M. Klein was a very different sort of man and poet. I say to the high school students who are reading this book and searching for comparisons between great Canadian poets: you're barking up the wrong maple tree there.

Abraham Moses Klein was born in Montreal to parents lucky enough and smart enough to have gotten out of Russia four years earlier in 1905. He was a brilliant student, graduating as a silver medalist from Baron Byng High School, the same place later immortalized (and immoralized) by **Mordecai Richler** in *The Apprenticeship of Duddy Kravitz* as "Fletcher's Field." Unlike the younger novelist, however, Klein didn't have a grandfather who was a rabbi to rebel against. Indeed, Klein actually studied for the rabbinate at one point, filling his writing with a love and understanding of his religion instead of petty rage, Freudian misunderstanding and childish viciousness.

Not that Klein remained religious, since he seemed to transfer much of his spiritual passion to Zionism as a teenager, before moving on to study at McGill University. Even as an undergraduate, he began to have his poems published in the *Canadian Forum* and elsewhere, before he recognized the impressive living that the five bucks a poem was promising him and enrolled in law school at the Université de Montréal. (To paraphrase an ancient Talmudic aphorism, "When the poetic muse calls and when the bar calls, better to answer the bar; you can always write poems on the side and not break your parents' hearts, as well as your banker's." Well, I *said* it was a paraphrase.)

In 1935, Klein married, and began to practise law in Noranda, Quebec, making him the most poetic, knowledgeably Jewish, myopic Zionist lawyer in that mining town at that time — in its entire history, in fact. It is interesting to note that Klein never found the legal profession either interesting or remunerative, which only goes to show what an honest, decent human being he was, in spite of the cruel parody of Klein as the poet L. B. Berger in Richler's latest novel, *Solomon Gursky Was Here*. Such an attack is not surprising, however. Blacks have been known to call one another "nigger" at times, so why shouldn't Montreal Jewish writers have the right to insult each other, as well? After all, if Klein had the gall to make his living writing speeches for a certain distillery owner and not to love the bad Hemingway-style prose of Richler's first few novels, it seems only fair that Mordecai kick Klein after he's dead, right?

Since Klein's poems kept being published in major magazines during the 1930s, earning up to ten dollars each — a 100 percent raise! — the poet ended up having to edit various Jewish magazines and newspapers to make ends meet. (It could have been worse. Many poets are actually forced to teach at universities and cope with reading their students' writing (see **Earle Birney**; **E. J. Pratt**, et al.). Talk about the suffering poet, will you?

In 1940, Klein's first book of poetry, *Hath Not a Jew*, was published. As it happened, the Jews hath, but not very much in Europe during that decade. *The Hitleriad* (Klein was against) and *Poems* (he was for) came out in 1944, the same year the poet briefly stood for election as a CCF (socialist) candidate in Montreal Cartier (he soon withdrew his name). Klein did eventually run for Parliament in 1949 on the CCF ticket, but suffered a crushing defeat.

The Rocking Chair and Other Poems was published in 1948, and won a Governor General's Award. In it Klein showed not only a magnificent poetic style, but also astonishing insight and sensitivity toward the French-Canadian experience in Quebec. Indeed, one feels from reading the book that if anyone could have sold the Meech Lake Accord to the rest of Canada, it would have been Klein.

His one novel was *The Second Scroll* (1951), a fascinating mixture of philosophy, Zionism, poetry and prose. By 1954, Klein had begun to slip into mental illness. Eventually he ceased to write, vanishing into his home, where he died in his sleep nearly two decades later. Of course, had Richler's *Gursky* been published earlier, it might have killed Klein off long before. Since many of the patterns in the plots of Richler's *St. Urbain's Horseman* and *Gursky* appear to have been inspired by Klein's *Second Scroll*, we see here a classic Canadian example of the modern Yiddish expression "gnawing on the hand that feeds you."

FROM *AUTOBIOGRAPHICAL*
(1951)

Out of the Jew-crowded streets of the Main
I tried to dream of a Zion far away

While Morty Richler acted quite insane
And searched for nasty things 'bout Jews to say.
I recall my family murmuring prayer
As 'round the table talk of God abounded
While Richler spoke of *shiksas'* underwear
And sensitive Jewish kids his gang had hounded.
I sing of pogroms, and all hatreds untrue
And fight against the killers of my folk
As Morty writes his distaste for the Jew
And gives them, more than Gentiles, angry pokes.
I cry from times of cruelty and woes
And work for justice to be done to all
While Richler, many daggers wildly throws:
Maims *goy*, but mostly David, Ruth and Saul.

ROBERT KROETSCH

(1927 –)

IF **Mavis Gallant** is Miss Paris, **Margaret Laurence** is Miss Manawaka, **Margaret Atwood** is Ms. Canada, **Alice Munro** is Miss Smalltown Canada and **Susanna Moodie** is Miss Nineteenth-century Canada, then Robert Kroetsch is Myth Canada. But what a stud.

ARCHIBALD LAMPMAN

(1861 – 1899)

LAMPMAN was born in a tiny town in Ontario, where his father was rector of a church. His mother was nearly the wrecker of the church, but they never tell you about that. Both his grandfathers were

United Empire Loyalists, making them either true Canadians or traitorous Americans, depending upon your point of view. At the tender age of seven, Lampman got rheumatic fever, making him a hot poet even before he had put a single word down on a page.

The future poet was educated at home in his early youth, but entered a private school in 1870, where he studied Greek and Latin, the two official languages of intellectual Canada at that time.

Lampman eventually ended up at Trinity College in Toronto, where he won several scholarships, even beating out a number of ancient Greeks and Romans, for whom Greek and Latin were their native tongues. He was not a particularly good student, however, and was known more as a drinker and a smoker.

Lampman did edit his school newspaper, though, an excellent opportunity for a future poet because he kept sneaking his writing in, passing it off as letters to the editor. He graduated in 1882 with only second-class honours in Classics. In Smoking 409 and Boozing 457, however, he was all As.

The next silly thing Lampman did was to teach high school in a village near Toronto for a few months, until he came to the realization that he didn't really fit in: he was unreliable, always late and kept losing his students' papers. These attributes moved him to join the Post Office Department in Ottawa, where he worked until his death. Rather, since this was the Civil Service, let's just say that he was on salary until his death.

Lampman married, and fathered two children, which was already pretty prolific for a budding Canadian poet. But raising children was considered women's work, and thus never done (by men); Lampman, in spite of his laughable given name, was one of the pre-Hemingway, macho types: when not sleeping off drunken binges at the post office, he spent most of his time taking his trusty canoe out on various lakes in the Ottawa area. It was on one of those solitary trips (at least that's what he told his wife) that he injured himself, finally dying a few short years later, in 1899.

And so, Archibald Lampman lived less than four decades. But, having spent the last seventeen years of his life in the nation's capital, it *seemed* like a century — as it does to read his poems. His books of verse include *Among the Millet*, published in 1888 and *not* a reference to Edna St. Vincent, and *Lyrics of Earth*, published in 1895. He was working on the galleys of a third book, *Alcyone*, when he left this mortal coil. But, then, working on a galley can do that, especially when one's health, like Lampman's, has never been too great.

FROM *THE CITY OF THE END OF THINGS* *(1899)*

Beside the frozen Rideau stream
There is a place that makes blood cold
'Tis filled with Living Dead who scream
And poltroons who act stately; bold
Vicious and petty are these men
Whom we elect like ding-a-lings
It has been called since who knows when
The City of the End of Things.
It was called Bytown, long ago
A place as innocent as saints
But as the Parliament doth grow
It each MP with great Evil taints
Whether Whig or whether Tory
Still corruption rules the town

From crooked lips, the same old story:
Claims of statesman; deeds of clown.
Heads of an accursed state,
Asses in the shape of kings.
All the Idiots rate
The City of the End of Things.

Margaret Laurence

(1926 – 1987)

For many years Canada's most successful novelist, Margaret Laurence was born Jean Margaret Wemys in a Manitoba town called Neepawa, although most people think it should be called Manawaka for some reason or other — actually, for lots of reasons.

Even as a child, the future Margaret Laurence decided to become a writer, which at that time was known as a death wish, since there were no grants, no greats and no greetings available to Canadian writers in the 1940s, much less decent livings. After graduating in Honours English from United College in Winnipeg, where the syllabus was so weak it contained no writings by Margaret Laurence, she

married a civil engineer and moved with him to England, then Africa. Although she would eventually become known as a regional writer, it was rare at this point in our country's literary history for those regions to include Somaliland and Ghana.

For more than sixteen years the young writer turned out stories, novels and memoirs about her experiences in Africa, including *A Tree for Poverty* (1954), *This Side Jordan* (1960) and *The Tomorrow-Tamer* (1963), even after she returned to Canada, having become its literary and literal Great White Hope.

Then, in 1964, came her first novel set in Manitoba, *The Stone Angel*, followed by more Manawaka books: *A Jest of God* (1966), which had the good fortune of starring Joanne Woodward in the movie version instead of Robert Redford, thereby avoiding his murdering Laurence's African stories as he did Isak Dinesen's; and *The Fire-Dwellers* (1969). There was even a collection of linked short stories, also set in her favourite Manitoba town, *A Bird in the House* (1970), which was worth two of anyone else's writing about the bush.

Over the years, Laurence became a sort of godmother for Canadian Literature, inspiring other writers, fighting for good causes (she was against nuclear war, which might not seem impressive until you recall how many politicians seem to be for it) and turning out several children's books, as well as her last major work of fiction, *The Diviners*, which most critics thought was too, too divine. In this latter complex and dense book, as in most of her best works of fiction, we live very much in the past. Now that Laurence is, sadly, gone, and no longer turning out her very impressive works, the past seems the wisest place to live, since then she was alive and writing.

THE PLOT OF *THE STONE ANGEL*

THIS BOOK IS PARTICULARLY interesting in that it takes place entirely inside the deteriorating mind of the protagonist, who is often an antagonist, and anti-others, and taking antacids, since she is ninety years old. This fact has tended to scare off the high school English students assigned this book over the past quarter century, but it shouldn't. They should only have grannies with the brains, guts, tenacity and poetic sensibility of Hagar Shipley.

Hagar has the misfortune of having the same name as the Hagar in the Bible, another book some kids today haven't heard about or read, because there are no Coles Notes on it. Hagar, of course, was the handmaid — actually, the right-handmaid — of Abraham in the book of Genesis, who was used as a portable womb by him when his own wife, Sarah, was barren. This probably didn't inspire **Atwood's** *Handmaid's Tale*, even though that was a very good book, too.

Hagar has become forgetful, something that could be fatal for a novel taking place in someone's memory, except that she is "rampant with memory," so we get lots of information: she lives with Marvin, her elder son, and his wife, Doris, who are also getting older and don't particularly enjoy taking care of an irascible, irritating old woman. Her son and daughter-in-law suggest taking her to a nursing home, "Silverthreads" — pretty symbolic, when you come to think of it — but she is horrified by the place and escapes to an abandoned fish cannery, which is getting pretty easy to do in the Maritimes nowadays.

Throughout *The Stone Angel*, we relive Hagar's self-denying, life-denying existence: her father's stifling pride, which echoes the family cry of "Gainsay Who Dare!"

(presumably warning the family against high caloric food); her growing up in Manawaka, which often makes apartheid look like social democracy; her refusal to share her affection and inner feelings with her husband, Bram, (as in Abraham — and he was married before to a Clara/Sarah, too); her lifelong rejection of her son Marvin and her passion for her son John, who fills her with a life of guilt when he drives headlong into a train, something highly improbable in Mulroney's Canada today; her deeply moving acceptance of her life, and Marvin, and Doris; her discovery that pride had been her "wilderness"; and, in the last moments of this stunning, heartbreaking, inspiring, exquisite novel, her acceptance of —

Irving Layton

(1912 –)

The messiah of Canadian poetry, the messiah of world literature and the Messiah Himself if we choose to take the title of his autobiography, *Waiting for the Messiah*, literally, since he was born without a foreskin (in Romania, after which his parents quickly rushed their wunderkind to Montreal when he was barely one). In her superior biography of Layton, Elspeth Cameron noted in passing that this occurrence is not very rare at all, and happens to about one in 700 baby boys (and to 100 percent of all baby girls, in point of fact). For this observation, among several others, Layton called Ms. Cameron "a cow," called her skills into question and called out his lawyers. They didn't have much to do.

Nevertheless Israel Lazarovitch, as he was first named, is one of this country's most controversial, talented, driven, passionate and brilliant poets, however outrageously uneven. For Canada, Layton has proven many things: that it is possible to write with your head between your legs; that it is possible to write about unmentionables even while mentioning them; that it is possible to write great poetry, sprinkled amongst poetry so stunningly awful it's hard to believe Jack McClelland would agree to publish it, except that he always did. (We'll have to ask Jack about this the next time we see him.)

For nearly five decades, Layton has been putting out volumes of poetry, for a total of more than two dozen, of which possibly four volumes have been worthy of being published. (*Why?* Jack. *Why?*) Among his finest collections — you can tell by the titles — are *The Improved Binoculars* (1956) and *A Red Carpet for the Sun* (1959). Some of his more descriptive titles, if not anthologies of particularly good poems, are *The Swinging Flesh* (1961) and *Balls for a One-armed Juggler* (1963), two titles only Irving Layton could have come up with.

Throughout his life, Layton has fought like a bantam (which never published his poetry, by the way) against the middle class (but who else purchased his poems?); against self-righteousness and sanctimoniousness (there goes the rest of his audience); and for sexual freedom (so long, Canada). He has always known how to get his fellow citizens' danders up, if not their wallets out: dedicating a book to Lyndon Baines Johnson because of his wonderful handling of the Vietnam War; supporting Trudeau's imposition of the War Measures Act; and several other winning moves.

Still, no one would deny that Irving Layton has been the pea in the princess's mattress (more like pee, in Layton's case); the thorn in the Canadian public's side; the flower of Canadian poetry (if too often its blooming idiot). Like the Girl Who Had a Little Curl in the famous nursery rhyme, when Layton is good he is astonishingly good (for example "The Birth of Tragedy," "Keine Lazarovitch," "Berry Picking," "The Fertile Muck," "The Cold Green Element," "Whatever Else, Poetry Is Freedom") and when he is bad he is awful.

For My Brother Jesus

Yes, sir! You're sure my brother, Jesus!
You were a Jew and I am a Jew, and we're all
brothers.
Of course, they killed millions of Jews in this
century
So they would have killed you, too, Jesus, had
You been alive.
Which is the whole point of this nonpoem.
Not too intellectually profound, I confess,
But it proves the goyim are a total mess.

from *Shakespeare*

My son asks me, digging in the knife,
"Who's the best poet?" (The bugger causes strife.)
"Shakespeare," I most reluctantly reply.
"Is he better than you?" (He can make me cry.)
"Yes," I find I have to admit,
(Even though the Bard never wrote "sh--"
Or "f---" or "b----" or "c---" or "s--"
Nor even, for that matter, *Oedipus Rex.*)

But if I write millions of poems, as clearly I'm
doin',

Even tho' it may lead to McClelland's ruin,*
Maybe I'll write that perfect poem,
And they'll invite me to perform at SkyDome.
'Cause Shakespeare's dead — and, without sounding shrewish,
You have to admit: he wasn't even Jewish.

STEPHEN LEACOCK

(1869 – 1944)

ONE of the few Canadian writers who have achieved worldwide reputation — indeed, until the 1970s, possibly the *only* Canadian writer who had achieved worldwide reputation — Stephen Leacock was born in Hampshire, England, in 1869. Which might be one reason that he achieved worldwide reputation. Alas, when he was only six, his parents brought him to Canada, hoping to leave him here. They settled in Ontario on a farm near Lake Simcoe, an area that would someday become famous as a suburb of Toronto.

Thanks to money sent over from relatives back in England, who didn't want the Leacocks to return, they managed to avoid starving while farming the richest land outside the Ukraine. Young Stephen was sent off to Upper Canada College and the University of Toronto, where he could have grown into a self-righteous, racist snob, but instead became the exact opposite: a good humorist.

Lacking direction in his life, Leacock returned to Upper Canada College and taught until 1899, when he went off to Chicago to do graduate work in economics and poli-

* It did.

tics — surely the two funniest subjects in Canadian history (for example, the monetary policies and career of Pierre Trudeau, 1968–1979 and 1980–1984).

By 1903, Leacock had had enough, so he took his doctorate and returned to the country that had been so good to him, allowing him to keep from starving on a farm and, later, to hang around with self-righteous, racist snobs, and become a lecturer in economics and political science at McGill University in Montreal.

It was every humorist's dream: a steady job; a secure position to fall back on; tenure; life insurance paid for; regular cheques deposited in his bank account.

Well, maybe every *Canadian*'s dream.

Anyway, Stephen Leacock had them rolling in the aisles with his first book, *Elements of Political Science*, in 1906. Unfortunately he had intended to write a serious book on political science. But the future for his humour pieces seemed wide open. And he could keep his day job, too.

Still, humour is serious business, as we all know, so Leacock kept churning out books on politics, economics and Canadian history, all as funny as their subject matter, which is pretty funny, at least unintentionally.

Eventually Leacock became widely known and admired as the writer of witty and comical sketches. His first book of intentional humour, *Literary Lapses*, was published in 1910, the same year that Mark Twain died. Of course, it was also the same year that Halley's comet visited Earth, and no one suggested that Halley's soul had somehow entered Leacock's body.

The books continued to pour from him like bad economic news from Ottawa: *Nonsense Novels* (1911), *Sunshine Sketches of a Little Town* (1912), *Arcadian Adventures with the Idle Rich* (1914). If Leacock hadn't had agreeable graduate students marking all his undergraduate papers at

McGill, who knows how many successful humorous essays might never have been written?

Anyway, many of his finest works were placed in the fictitious Ontario town of Mariposa, which, as everyone in the world now knows, is actually the equally fictitious town of Orillia, Ontario, better known currently as the birthplace of Gordon Lightfoot, the factious folk-singer who is so popular in the real world today.

In order to commemorate the remarkable career and equally remarkable skills of this remarkable economist, Canada has responded in the ways it knows best. On the political level, Canadian elected officials have worked, on both the federal and provincial scenes, to make the economy of this country the laughing-stock of North America and the world. On the educational level, teachers from Newfoundland to British Columbia have gone out of their way to seek out particularly unfunny Leacock essays to teach to their reluctant students, helping to turn them against their country's writers for life. And, most touchingly, the city of Orillia set up a foundation, with the help of some whiskey brewer or other, to award the Leacock Award for Humour every year, usually for "the least funny book written by a Canadian during the previous twelve months." Which is a pretty funny concept, you'll have to admit.

My Financial Career

WHENEVER THIS COUNTRY has anything to do with banks, it gets rattled. The members of Parliament rattle it. The sight of money rattles it. Everything rattles it.

The moment the Canadian government tries to get involved with banks and attempts to transact business with one, it becomes an irresponsible idiot.

Of course, banking has brought success and wealth to

thousands of bankers, right through our history. From dispossessing Canadian widows and orphans of their homes, to sustaining military dictatorships around the world in their struggle against godless communism, banking remains a crucial part of this nation's heritage. But, then, so are charging Chinese Canadians a head tax and electing to higher office lunatics who talk to dead dogs and deader mothers.

Many banks opened their doors to unsuspecting customers in the early years of the past century, but only one survived: the Bank of Montreal, which opened in 1817 and has been closing accounts ever since. It was the inspired idea of a group of merchants in that great French city, who had no idea that the future of banking lay in Toronto, with the Anglos.

The Montreal Bank, as it was then known, as well as other banks that were popping up across Canada like so many weeds, issued their own banknotes, which allowed for fabulous profits. Sadly a central bank would open in Ottawa in 1935 and ruin much of their fun. By the year Canada became a confederation there were thirty-five banks in eastern Canada, then known as British North America. Who knew at the time that these banks, stuck way up north in Canada, would someday make Brazil safe for poverty and drug running?

In the early nineteenth century, a bank was often nothing more than a tent in which the bank manager slept each night with the bank's money under his pillow and a revolver next to him. Today, many decades later, wise Canadians keep their *own* money under *their* pillows and carry a revolver whenever they visit a bank.

Or they should, just in case they get rattled.

Customers back then had limited need for the services of their friendly neighbourhood bank. Canadians didn't get around that much, since the horse was often in the garage or was always riding off in all directions. Most Canadians didn't like to borrow, either, being uptight WASPs, and they would simply use overdrafts as a kind of loan. The federal government in Ottawa would later take up that tradition. And, back in the last century, most Canadians bartered, rather than use cash — just as in most Canadian trades today.

Canada's banks have helped their citizens to become rattled. They have loaned money to many of this country's entrepreneurs, often at usurious rates that would make Shylock drool, and then eagerly sold off the borrowers' furniture, houses and children when the businesses did not succeed. The chartered banks have also helped meet the financial needs of hydro, lumber, mining, fossil, agricultural and so many other companies, by lending money to American firms, who would then take the Canadian businesses over, happily paying back the Canadian banks. This is known as God-fearing capitalism.

Banks have affected Canada in social ways, as well. For instance, they have tended to keep women out of power, or any directorship, in any bank. The reason for this is clear, and it need not be antifeminism: you see, bankers know that no intelligent woman would *ever* lend tens of billions of dollars to South American dictatorships, which is what keeps most of the banks busy.

There are many moral questions that arise in the world of banking. For instance, how does a bank repossess a fascist state? Is there a way to merely repossess their weather, without having to take all their lousy poor? Is the answer to charge twenty-one percent interest on current account overdrafts in Red Deer and 29.5 percent on VISA accounts in Whitney Pier?

To help them out of their predicament, Canada's banks

hope to get into new and more exciting things: car leasing, stockbroking, oil-and-lube jobs, dry cleaning, life insurance. The only thing banks won't be willing to sell is shirts, since they lost those in bad loans to Central American drug dealers many years ago.

In the meantime, I propose that we bank no more. I personally suggest keeping your money in cash in a pants pocket and your savings in silver dollars in a sock.

DENNIS LEE

(1939 –)

ONE of the country's favourite children's poets, Dennis Lee suffers from the same agony as fellow millionaire Raffi, who also began as a "singer" for adults but found his future usurped by the Pampers generation.

Born in Toronto the first year of World War II, Lee attended the University of Toronto, earning both his B.A. and M.A., and taught there for several years. Then he helped found some of the major hippie-dippie institutions of the 1960s, including Rochdale College and the House of Anansi Press, both of which went to pot literally. Of these experiences he wrote:

Lovely Rochdale school
Lovely Rochdale school
Love to love and smoke some dope
And make cops play the fool.
Helped create Anansi,
Publishing's real cool —
But sex and dope and rock is best
At lovely Rochdale school.

Lee served as an editor for various major Canadian publishers, including Macmillan and McClelland and Stewart, while working as a poet and critic. Although he wrote many fine poems, especially his collection *Civil Elegies*, which eventually won a Governor General's Award for poetry in 1972, Lee found himself caught in a day-care centre of culture: Kid Lit.

Indeed, not only did Lee turn out book after book after book of rollicking children's poetry, ranging from *Wiggle to the Laundromat* to *Alligator Pie* to *Nicholas Knock* to *Garbage Delight*, all published in the 1970s, he reached his peak in the early 1980s as the creator of song lyrics for *Fraggle Rock*, answering the question that has troubled every great poet from Homer to Milton to Donne to Eliot to Lowell: can a serious poet find peace with the Muppets? The answer was soon clear, as expressed in Lee's own "Lovesong of J. Alfred Kidwriter":

Writing for the mob
Is an easy job
Sure pays lots of money
More than for *The Gods.*
Take away the Council grants
And lit'rary hobnob
There's more bucks than imagined
From writing for the mob.

FROM *GARBAGE DELIGHT*

I'm not exactly talented
    And not exactly dumb,
But writing rhymes for little kids
    Keeps me in the rum.

Some poets like to write tough things
    And challenge everyone.
But writing rhymes for little kids
    Makes bucks by the ton.

And then I like to settle down
    And poof: I'm Father Goose.
'Cause no one bought *Harold Ladoo*
    Which used creative juice.

I've thought about it in my mind:
    Selling out, I mean —
And now I like it best, because
    My name's on TV screens!

Dennis Had a Talent

Dennis had a talent,
    A talent,
    A talent,
Dennis had a talent,
    And Leonard taped some songs.

Dennis looked peculiar,
    Peculiar,
    Peculiar,
Dennis looked peculiar,
    And Leonard sounded wrong.

Dennis turned to kid-stuff,
    Kid-stuff,
    Kid-stuff,
Dennis turned to kid-stuff,
    While Leonard's poems seared.

Now Dennis just writes smooth things,
    Easy things,
    Soft things,
Dennis writes for Muppets now,
    While Cohen is revered.

ROGER LEMELIN

(1919 –)

THE proof is in *Les Plouffe*.

DOROTHY LIVESAY

(1909 –)

SURE, it helped to have a father and a mother who were both newspaper journalists back in the days when reporters could actually have a style. And sure, it helped to be born in Winnipeg, where you've got to keep writing in order to keep the ink from freezing. And sure, it helped to be a socialist and a social worker and care about women and blacks and the poor and the downtrodden, even when the governments of Canada never did. And sure, it helped to be a passionate woman and a passionate feminist, even though she was both long before either was acceptable in Canada. Still, none of those things guaranteed that she'd turn out to be such a wonderful poet.

MALCOLM LOWRY

(1909 – 1957)

THE man who singlehandedly turned heavy drinking into art is also the man whose Canadian content was the greatest stretch until Danny

DeVito auditioned for the role of Magic Johnson a third of a century after Malcolm Lowry died.

Let me explain.

Lowry was born just outside Liverpool, England, which we assume makes the Beatles ripe for being claimed by Canada, as well. His father was a wealthy cotton salesman, so the lad was educated in some of the finest boarding schools in England (despite this, however, he turned out heterosexual). Since his brothers all went into the family business, and since he had a gift for jazz songwriting, Lowry knew he had to escape somehow. But where? What place would bring his family the greatest hurt and humiliation? A bordello? Pittsburgh? No, not cruel enough. So he hired on as a cabin boy on a freighter heading for the China coast. (This was done under the influence of reading too much Eugene O'Neill, who was usually under the influence, anyway.)

Then, tired of world travel and sufficiently broadened, although still not Canadian enough for future scholars to claim him for this country, Lowry returned to England in order to become Canadian enough for future scholars to claim him for this country. After writing his first novel, *Ultramarine*, about some of his experience on the (usually) high seas, he entered classes at Cambridge. There he came into contact with numerous writers, picking up God knows how many communicable diseases. He graduated in 1932, just in time for the Great Depression, which was more than ready for him.

Lowry had considerable problems with *Ultramarine*, and only partially because the sole copy vanished from the automobile of an editor (an excuse we recommend to all future writers and editors). It appears that the young writer — and the older writer, for that matter — suffered from a chronic inability to complete, to his own satisfaction, any manuscript much larger than a breadbox. This made bread hard to come by, and his literary output during his lifetime — usually the most prolific period of time for writers — extremely slight. In retrospect, this was all right. His desk and shelves tended to be too covered with empty and half-empty liquor bottles to leave any room for manuscripts, anyway.

For most of the 1930s, Lowry lived in France, the United States and Mexico, his time rapidly running out if he wanted to be considered one of Canada's greatest authors. But, thank heavens, he managed to stagger, bottle in hand, up to Dollarton, just outside Vancouver, in 1939, staying for fifteen years, a period of time that was just long enough to qualify him to win the Governor General's Award for fiction in 1961, long after he had split from his brief home and briefly chosen native land, for his collection of short stories, *Hear Us O Lord from Heaven Thy Dwelling Place.* (Even the title went through two dozen drafts and took him five years to write.)

While in Canada — which makes him One of Ours for eternity — Lowry and his second wife lived in a squatter's shack on a beach bordering the Pacific Ocean, which was sold by another squatter in 1987 for over $725,000. It was a very special house, since it was made entirely out of empty liquor bottles and wine flasks, leading to his winning the Governor General's Award for Recycling in 1953. It was in this lovely little shack that Lowry managed to complete the third version of *Under the Volcano*, which he had been working on for only a decade or so — pretty fast for him.

Canada had a profound effect on Lowry's art — after all, wasn't Seagram's a local specialty? — as did his brief stays in Oakville and Niagara-on-the-Lake, Ontario. The harsh and cruel liquor laws of the latter sent the budding artist back to Mexico for a second time. He ended up in prison there, then went to Haiti, where, after years in the red, he ended up in the black. His wife was furious.

In 1954, Lowry, his angry wife and several cases of hooch left Canada for an extended trip to the Old Country. Soon after their departure Lowry's chosen country showed its affection for him by expropriating the land next to his beach slum, thus taking his shack away from him. *You can't go home again*, thought Lowry, even though the line had already been used. He continued to rewrite and redrink everything while wandering across Europe, until his death in England, in 1957. Not surprisingly, the cause of death was an overdose of alcohol and barbiturates, a combination that had always inspired him far better in the past.

Lowry's entire life was a blur of paranoia and alcoholism, although it is actually unfair to accuse him of paranoia, since all those pink elephants and monstrous editors actually *were* after him. But, thank God, he lived in Canada long enough for us to claim him. Most critics of this country will never forgive Saul Bellow's parents for leaving suburban Montreal for Chicago when the future author was only nine, or Bellow himself for actually managing to win the Nobel Prize for Literature, an award Canada would really like to have, even if given to an old British drunk who lived here for only a few years.

FROM *UNDER THE VOLCANO*

MARVELOUS," SAID THE CONSUL, raising the drink to his lips.

Yvonne pointed to Popocatapetl once more, daring the consul to pronounce it.

"For that, I'll need a drink," he replied, picking up the bottle of tequila and downing it all.

"Did you know that today is Peter Lorre's birthday?" she asked him, smiling.

"Really?" the consul replied, gritting his teeth. "Hell, I'll drink to that."

Which he did.

The consul then tried to pronounce the name of the volcano he would make famous, but found that he needed another drink or two or three to get his lips around it.

"Boy, I sure needed that," said the consul with a smile, downing several bottles of Mexican rum. "Now, lemme try it again. Pop-o-cat-a-pet . . . Yep, cats *are* pets, aren't they?"

"So how's that hangover, Dad?" asked Yvonne, grinning.

"What hangover?" the consul exploded angrily, face down on the barroom floor. "I *never* drink very much before eight in the morning."

"It's 7:35 a.m.," his daughter replied, disappointed.

"Not in Pittsburgh," he defended himself, reaching up for another bottle. "Anyway, I shall never drink again. Nevermore."

The two climbed aboard the old rickety bus that would take them both up the highly symbolic mountain, which now looked strangely attractive in the mountain, er, morning dew. It looked, in fact, like a giant bottle of Château Inebriate 1934, which happened to be a very good year.

"*Every* year of Château Inebriate is a very good year," the consul said aloud to no one in particular, while reaching over and grabbing the bottle of tequila from the shaky hand of the drunken driver of the bus, then downing it.

"I thought you said you'd never drink again," said Yvonne, teasing him sweetly, tweaking his nose and having a few slugs herself when he wasn't looking.

"That was before we got on the bus," the consul snapped, as the vehicle rolled uncertainly toward the highly symbolic volcano. "I'm older and wiser now, and more travelled, so I can handle my drinks better. At least I'm not driving."

"Oh, look at that profoundly symbolic jungle out there!" squealed his daughter, staring out the dirty window of the bus.

"Hell, I'll drink to that," said the consul, sliding slowly but steadily off his seat into the aisle of the bus, while grabbing a sadly only three-quarters full bottle of tequila from the young pregnant Mexican woman sitting next to him and finishing it off. "You shouldn't drink when you're preggers," he admonished her, "and you certainly should *not* be sharing a bottle with a strange man."

"No comprende, señor," the young woman said, smiling enigmatically, if not symbolically.

"Nada," murmured Yvonne. *"Nada, nada, nada."*

"Here's to the Dominion of Ca-*nada*!" said the consul with a chuckle, taking another swig and then briefly passing out in the shadow of the most symbolic mountain ever known to mankind, whether sober or not, but mainly not.

Gwendolyn MacEwen

(1941 – 1987)

An early talent, an early mythologizer, an early brilliance, a far, far too early death.

Hugh MacLennan

(1907 –)

Known as the author who has done for Protestants what **Mordecai Richler** has done for Jews, Hugh MacLennan was born in 1907 in the mining town of Glace Bay, on Cape Breton Island. His father was a doctor, and both parents were Scottish (his mother was a McQuarrie), so he really couldn't have failed at anything he chose to do with his life, provided he stayed in Canada and got out of Cape Breton. He did both, and didn't fail, even if many of the turgid plots of his endless novels did.

In 1917, while a grade five student in a Halifax school, the young lad saw and heard the devastating explosion of a munitions ship in the city's harbour. One of his teachers was badly cut by flying glass, upon which the bright, responsible young MacLennan was heard to say, "I had nothing to do with it." So maybe he wasn't responsible, after all.

As a teenager, MacLennan attended Dalhousie University in Halifax, which had unfortunately survived the blast of several years earlier. He not only studied Classics and did brilliantly, but was also a star in many collegiate sports, including tennis and basketball, frequently at the same time, something that confused the judges no end. Often combining his brilliance in each, young Hugh used to scream, "Fifteen-Agape!" and "We beat those lousy barbarians, CXIV to LXXIX!"

A gifted student, MacLennan graduated with honours and won a Rhodes Scholarship to study at Oxford University, an institute of higher learning to the east of Dalhousie. By 1932, he returned, clutching an Honour Mods from Oxford, only to discover that in the Great Depression, things had gone rockers. And when he saw an Englishman with the same qualifications as his get the only teaching job at his alma mater, he realized that being 100 percent Scottish, even in Nova Scotia, still wasn't as good as being 100 percent English, at least in the Canada of the 1930s. (You can imagine what the chances of future theatre critic Nathan Cohen were, growing up during this same time in Whitney Pier, just outside Sydney.)

MacLennan wouldn't take this affront sitting down, so

he stood up and moved down to the States, where he obtained his Ph.D. in 1935, with a thesis entitled *Oxyrhynchus*, a study of an ancient Roman city in Egypt. It sold even fewer copies than many of his later novels.

At this time, other important changes took place in the life of Hugh MacLennan: he moved to Montreal, where he began to teach Latin and history at a college, got married and fell in love with his new city. He thought his new wife was okay, too, and even wrote about her in lots of books.

During the Second World War, MacLennan volunteered to fight for Canada, but was rejected on medical grounds. This happened to **Robertson Davies**, as well, and his novels are much more fun, so I'm not certain what to make of this. Anyway, MacLennan could have been killed, and then we would never have experienced the excitement of *Each Man's Son* and other classics. Clearly the Allies managed without him.

In 1941, MacLennan published his first novel, *Barometer Rising*, a book that has moved hundreds of thousands of Canadian high school students to shell out several bucks for a Coles Notes on it ever since. Most people feel the author was just using the great Halifax explosion of 1917 to symbolize the huge upheaval taking place in Canada over the country's status as a colony, but all those people discovered this in Coles Notes, since the book itself doesn't make it particularly clear. In the novel, Colonel Wain is killed and most of the older parts of the city are destroyed, while the younger characters come through without a scratch. This is probably symbolic, too, but you'll have to check your own Coles Notes to see if you agree.

Over the next four decades, the regular flow from the pen of Hugh MacLennan would fill Canadian high school students with anticipation, despair and horror. *Two Solitudes* was published in 1945, giving this country a new phrase for its English/French divisions, when most scholars had thought it had come from Rilke. Within a generation, the novel was translated into a dozen languages, a purported movie and hundreds of thousands of dollars of further profit for the publishers of Coles Notes.

More books kept coming, each more difficult to read than the one before: *The Precipice* in 1948; *Each Man's Son* in 1951; *The Watch That Ends the Night* in 1959; *The Return of the Sphinx* in 1967; and many others too numerous and painful to mention, including *Voices in Time* (1980), in which Montreal is annihilated in a nuclear holocaust, making Bill 101 ultimately irrelevant.

Although MacLennan's writing career has been filled with Governor General's Awards galore (which should not be held against him), possibly his greatest moment came with the release, then quick disappearance, of a film of *Two Solitudes* in 1978 (it might have had a chance had it been renamed *Sex, Drugs and Rock 'n' Roll*). This movie version of MacLennan's most famous book, all about religious, cultural and national tensions in Quebec, while filmed on location, was directed by Britisher Lionel Chetwynd, and starred American Stacy Keach as Huntly McQueen and Parisian Jean-Pierre Aumont as Athanase Tallard. One can only assume these two actors were chosen because Eddie Murphy was too expensive to play McQueen and Meryl Streep had other commitments and so was unavailable to play Athanase. With luck, the film will never come out on video.

ANTONINE MAILLET

(1929 –)

ACADIAN Adventures with the Never Idle Poor.

CHARLES MAIR

(1938 – 1927)

CHARLES Mair was born in Lanark, in Upper Canada, but lived much of his nearly nine decades out West, even before anyone knew oil was out there. Until the precious fuel was discovered, there was still nothing of value to be found in the West.

As a young man, Mair briefly studied medicine at Queen's University in Kingston, but left in 1857 to work in his family's timber business for the next decade, where he would be able to do far less damage. After managing to complete a second year of studies, he was off to Ottawa, where he became one of the founders of the Canada First movement. This was eventually changed to the America First movement, following the 1984 federal Tory landslide.

As a paymaster out in the Red River settlement — today's Winnipeg, but just as cold in 1869 — his letters were printed in the Toronto *Globe*. In them he heaped praise upon the land, and garbage on the native Indians, especially the women — just as federal politicians would do, more than a century later. Mair was thanked personally by the great rebel Louis Riel, who captured and imprisoned the poet in 1870, sentencing him to death. Had the hanging actually occurred, future scholars would have been spared countless hours of poetic injustice. But Mair escaped from Fort Garry, made his way back East, rallied the public against the mighty Métis and returned west to help suppress Riel's Northwest Rebellion of 1885. Only years later did the public learn that what *really* upset Mair was that Riel had stolen his poems. In any case, Mair's execution of his poetry was far less successful than Sir John A.'s execution of Louis Riel.

Mair's first book was *Dreamland and Other Poems*

(1868), which was loved by every critic who hadn't read Keats or Whitman yet. Indeed, he was dubbed "the warrior bard" because of his struggle against Riel. The public, however, was soon "wearier, bored."

Eventually Mair moved to Windsor, Ontario, presumably to be close to Detroit so he could escape the wrath of his readers. In 1886, he wrote a verse play about the War of 1812, entitled *Tecumseh: A Drama* (Pierre Berton would do it better). Most scholars assume he tacked on "A Drama" to let people know what they were reading.

Mair finally died in Victoria, British Columbia, but since it *was* Victoria, no one noticed that he had passed away until a number of years later. His problematic career wasn't all his fault, however. Since he spent so much of his life in the far West (Windsor, Winnipeg), he was out of touch with many of the exciting literary developments taking place in eastern Canada. Furthermore, his fax didn't work. This meant that his poetry was even more turgid than that of Roberts, Lampman and the other Canadian giants of the nineteenth century.

JOHN MCCRAE

(1872 – 1918)

ALTHOUGH not a veterinarian, John McCrae was born in Guelph in 1872. But he did study medicine at the University of Toronto and was a successful doctor in Montreal at a time when an Anglo still had a fighting chance.

McCrae served in the South African War, years before Canadians were to have nothing to do with South Africa and even more years before the Bank of Nova Scotia finally pulled its assets out.

Although the poem wasn't very funny at all, *Punch* magazine was the first to publish McCrae's most famous work, "In Flanders Fields," in 1915. Never a man to be shot, the young poet died of pneumonia in France in 1918, nearly seven full decades before that illness became a euphemism for AIDS.

In Flanders Fields

In Flanders fields the poppies grow
Then turn to opium, just so
 The public can obtain their highs
 And feel like flying through the skies
While crooks with guns hide out below.

We are the stoned. Short years ago
We lived and loved, our lawns did mow,
 Loved dope, were dopes, yet still we long
 for Flanders fields.

Take up the fight with our foe:
Those idiots who cry "Just say no!"
 We love the rush; so join us in our high.
 And if by chance we all may die
We shall not stop, while poppies grow
 In Flanders fields.

Marshall McLuhan

(1911 – 1980)

A devout Catholic in both meanings of the word, Marshall McLuhan is the most famous Canadian of the century, which, sadly, is still not saying much. But since Tom Wolfe (an American!) once compared him to Newton, Freud and Darwin, and he once had a brief role in a Woody Allen movie as a New York Jewish intellectual, this is good enough for most of us.

Born in modest circumstances in Edmonton, which is a redundancy, he had an ambitious mother and a henpecked father, something *de rigueur* in Canada, and most of the world, it seems. He was raised in Winnipeg and educated at the University of Manitoba (there's an oxymoron for you). After winning a scholarship to Cambridge, he became interested in advertising, a subject that was to haunt his thinking and his works for the rest of his life, as well as guarantee him cleaner pores, firmer dentures and the shiniest kitchen floor in Toronto. It was at this time that he converted to Catholicism.

After teaching at a number of midwestern U.S. colleges from 1936 to 1944, where he was the only Catholic within 500 miles in any direction, he had the presumption to teach at Assumption (later the University of Windsor), ending up at St. Mike's College at the University of Toronto, where he was a professor of English but secretly a guru of Communications, until his death on the last day of 1980. (He had always tended to put things off until the last minute, especially with the world expressing itself at the speed of light all the time.)

McLuhan soon got hot on the trail of the meaning of technology, while leaving his English students cold. Indeed, a taped lecture of one of his classes in the 1960s began as follows:

"Good morning, students. Today's lesson, as you know, is on James Joyce, about which we should rejoice. Not like the villain in last night's "Gunsmoke," who was shot down in the street, not to mention the heart. How many of you saw that episode? Only four? The rest of you fail. Which is fine, really, because young people today are after jobs, not careers. Education is *not* what you want, even though the word comes from the Latin word *ducare*, meaning to lead. But lead to what? TV and rock music, along with the political resurrection of Richard Nixon, is what's really important, so why sit in a classroom at all? Indeed, the city itself is a classroom without walls, as are movies, radio and TV, which is why "Gunsmoke" is so important. And speaking of important writers, have you done your reading of E. M. Forster, or have you only connected — that's a literary joke, folks — with Orwell, who created Orwellian material, while Forster couldn't see the forster through the trees. Not that trees are relevant anymore, since they once were basic to the publication of books, which are no longer read because of the rise of technology. Anyway, take out your T. S. Eliot — no relation to George, who wasn't even a guy, anyway — and open to anywhere you like, since individual pages have become obsolete. Yes, uh, Mr. Marchand, I believe?"

Young student in back. "Will this be on the exam?"

You get the idea.

McLuhan's first major book was *The Mechanical Bride: Folklore of Industrial Man*, in 1951, in which he made fun of the very popular culture of which he would soon become a major fixture. He poked fun at the way the human personality had become mechanized, and dissected newspaper and magazine advertisements with a fine-tooth comb, which he had purchased through a mail-order house, mainly because it was new and improved.

His most earth-shattering books were yet to come, first *The Gutenberg Galaxy: The Making of Typographic Man* (1962), in which McLuhan analyzed the culture of the world before Jack McClelland changed everything, and how the print culture changed our values with its moveable type, mass production of books and Canada Council grants. Unable to understand a word of it, the governor general gave it a special Incomprehensible Award in that year. This was the book that gave the world the phrase "global village," which has been misused in villages around the globe ever since.

Next came *Understanding Media: The Extensions of Man* (1964), wherein the now famous genius of technology studied the major changes in human responses brought about by electronics. Bought by millions of people and read by dozens, this was the book that gave the phrase "the medium is the message" to the world, which has been trying to give it back ever since. McLuhan went ahead and rephrased it as "The medium is the massage," "The medium is the mass-age," "The madam is a mess," "The modicum of a misogynist" and too many others even to mention. This confused the governor general all the more, when all he was usually expected to do was cut ribbons at opening ceremonies at hospitals, events McLuhan had insisted were no longer relevant without a CAT scan and other electronic breakthroughs.

McLuhan followed those three books with several thousand more, all written with (or by) others and most of them filled with lots of pix and large fonts so the inspired, brain-dead children of the television generation would be able to understand them.

Few will argue that McLuhan changed the world's way of looking at technology and the mass media, even though few have managed to understand him except his wife, Corinne, his six precocious children and about fifteen of his many millions of admirers. Thankfully, Woody Allen's *Annie Hall* came along (McLuhan had the starring role, according to McLuhan) to help him to live forever in the collective, global-villaged mind of this planet. Luckily most people have forgotten that this same man wrote: "English Canada is the most apathetic and unenthusiastic territory in all creation"; "There is no serious writing going on in Canada today — by anybody"; and "Stuff it, Northrop!" (the last being one of the many witticisms he uttered during his lengthy tenure on the U. of T. campus).

FROM *THE MECHANICAL GALAXY: MEDIUM, SINCE NOT RARE OR WELL DONE*

YES, WE'VE COME A LONG WAY, baby, and no wonder — and no wander, either, albeit sidewinder at times. If it weren't for the phonograph, those long-playing records wouldn't work at all, which is why the telegraph, unlike the telephone, extends and amplifies the voice, or maybe vice versa. Vice, of course, came with the invention of photography, with a new ability to reproduce some pretty hot pictures, especially for a Catholic. And versa would still be written, although without the same magnitude or relevancy to a plugged-in, turned-on, tuning-out generation.

This might be a good place to explain the terms "hot" and "cool," since as everyone knows, *Some Like It Hot* was a cool movie, while its box-office success was hot, which only adds to the confusion.

Did you hear (or, in this case, read) the one about the great film director who dies and goes to heaven after a long and exhausting career in Hollywood? After a few weeks of rest, Saint Peter approaches him — I'm a religious Catholic, don't forget — and asks him to direct a movie in heaven.

"No more pictures," he says.

"But the new script is by Shakespeare!" cries Saint Peter.

"Wow! But no, I'm just too tired. Forget it."

"And the original musical score is being written by Mozart."

"No kidding? Still, I've had a long career, and I want to rest for a few centuries."

"But the costumes and sets are being built by Michelangelo!"

"Hold on a minute," replies the great, if late, director. "Shakespeare? Mozart? Michelangelo? Okay, I'll make the film, after all."

"Great!" says Saint Peter. "But just one thing. God has got this little bimbo who *thinks* she can sing. . . . "

Now, why did I relay this obviously lengthy joke to you, when I have spent my life insisting that jokes in the late twentieth century have become shorter and shorter due to our instantaneous modes of technology and electronics? I'm not sure, but I'll check my notes and get back to you.

Anyway, back to hot and cool. You see, television is a cool medium, since it requires a great deal of input on the part of the viewer to put together all those teeny-tiny little dots one by one. Whereas radio is a hot medium, since it has a very high definition, by which I mean that it is overflowing with data.

No, wait a second. It's the other way around. It's radio that's cool, since you're just listening to it, while television is hot, because its commercials are in colour.

No, let's try the other way around again. TV is cool even though it's not so hot, while radio is hot, even though the CBC is rarely listened to except for Gzowski and Barbara Frum, who will never make it on television.

I trust you have that straight now. And if you do, I'd really appreciate it if you'd help *me* understand it. Just write to me at the Centre for Culture and Technology, Queen's College Circle, University of Toronto, Toronto, Canada. On second thought, it's better to phone, since writing has fallen by the wayside, what with the explosion of electronics, and no one reads anymore. So why do I write books then, you ask? There's a book in *that*, or maybe a videotape. I'll have to line up someone to help me put one together. . . .

W. O. MITCHELL

(1914 –)

"W.O." — as in "Whoa, don't write so quickly, please" — Mitchell was born and raised in Weyburn, Saskatchewan, a community even less interesting than Regina. At the age of twelve, the boy contracted bovine tuberculosis, which presumably comes from having cows cough all over you and which rarely occurs in major metropolitan areas. This led his widowed mother to take the future writer down to Florida, where the cows have less cause to catch colds.

After attending high school in St. Petersburg, Mitchell travelled across the States and eventually chose to study medicine at the University of Manitoba, determined to save the next generation from the disease that struck him down so tragically and forced him to live down in the U.S., where everyone has guns, is racist and experiences better weather. Sadly, he became sick once more, and left Manitoba to travel across Europe, finally settling in Seattle, where he avoided cows like the plague — and cows with the plague, for that matter.

Eventually Mitchell completed both undergraduate and education degrees at the University of Alberta, and began to teach school in rural Alberta, determined to learn to accept cows without bitterness or prejudice. By this time, Mitchell was writing plays, journalistic articles and fiction, even though no one had asked for him to do so. By 1944, barely in his thirtieth year, he had been published in magazines such as *Maclean's*, and in respected American magazines such as the *Atlantic Monthly*. This moved Mitchell to decide to give up his day job and move to High River, Alberta, where he would be inspired by the thrilling birth, inspiring childhood and dynamic youth of a future prime minister of Canada, the Right Honourable Joseph P. Clark, who would rule over this great land in the late 1970s and early 1980s. (We'd like to thank the federal Progressive Conservative Party for their generous sponsorship of the previous sentence, which helped to pay for the publication of this book.)

In 1947, W. O. Mitchell wrote his most successful work, *Who Has Seen the Wind*. (He never achieved the same success over the next forty-plus years, and in this sense, he was a lot like fellow Albertan Joe Clark, who also came from High River and who also peaked at a young age.) Within a year, Mitchell was fiction editor of *Maclean's*, a position no less important today, even after it became a newsmagazine several years ago.

For nearly a decade following this, Mitchell wrote many of the weekly scripts for his extremely popular "Jake and the Kid" radio series on CBC, at a precious time in this nation's history, when people still listened to radio and when people still listened to the CBC. Experiencing these touching, sentimental, obvious, sentimental, sanctimonious and sentimental radio programmes today, in the 1990s, makes one realize just how much the Canadian taste has improved over the past third of a century. (A collection of short stories with the same name won the Stephen Leacock Medal for Humour in 1962, and for the same reason that all other recipients of this revered prize have won it: the stories were sweet, sentimental and not particularly funny, so as not to threaten the memory of the sweet, sentimental, occasionally funny short stories of the award's namesake.)

By this time, Mitchell was being frequently compared with Mark Twain. This is quite remarkable, since Twain could be biting, savagely satirical, bitter, raging, and was possibly the greatest American novelist of the previous century, while W. O. Mitchell was sentimental, innocent and, being Canadian, *nice.*

A highly prolific, speedy writer, Mitchell quickly followed *Who Has Seen the Wind* (No, the "Who" in the title did *not* refer to Joe Clark) with the 1962 novel *The Kite* and the 1981 novel *How I Spent My Summer Holidays.* Would that new Canadian taxes came as frequently. All Mitchell's novels and plays make it clear that his childhood memories of the Canadian prairies made a far deeper impression on him than did his teenage years in St. Petersburg, Florida. We have only the cows of Weyburn, Saskatchewan to thank for that.

THE STORY OF *WHO HAS SEEN THE WIND*

LIKE NOBEL PRIZEWINNING novelist William Golding's *Lord of the Flies* and Mark Twain's *The Adventures of Huckleberry Finn*, Mitchell's novel is about growing up. Of course, the Golding book is about the evil in all of us and the Twain novel is about evil in the world, while Mitchell's opus is about a Canadian prairie boy who learns about life and death and intolerance, but other than that, they're really a lot alike. For instance, there are flies in the Golding work, and flies in Mitchell's. And there are dogs and rabbits in both the Twain and Mitchell books. So maybe *Who Has Seen the Wind* is better than both of them put together. And maybe Saskatoon has a more exciting night life than Montreal.

Through Mitchell's novel, we follow the growth and maturation of Brian O'Connal, who is just a young boy at the start, though he talks, thinks and acts like a thirty-two-year-old novelist from Weyburn, Saskatchewan who spent part of his youth in the southern United States. This just goes to show how quickly prairie kids grow up in western Canada.

There are many highlights in this warmhearted novel: little Brian's dog is killed; a gopher is tortured viciously by a group of boys; his good friend loses his rabbits; and his father and grandfather both die. Nowadays a prairie child would blame all these tragedies on Quebec or Ottawa, but back in the 1930s, when the novel takes place, all these trials and tribulations had to lead to a growing understanding of life and the inevitability of death. Clearly, Canada hasn't come a very long way at all.

Countless other earth-shattering events take place in the novel: young Brian must confront Mrs. Abercrombie's intolerance, the fanaticism of Mr. Powelly, the wise, shoemaking Milt Palmer and the kindly, perceptive school principal, Mr. Digby. It's enough to make one want to move to Toronto. Or maybe Buffalo.

By the end of the novel, the reader is sad to discover that young Brian will not go the way of all dogs, rabbits and grandparents, but has actually matured into the kind of sensitive, thoughtful, goody-goody type who may someday write sentimental, caricatured, soft novels about growing up on the Prairies. For this, alas, science has still discovered no cure.

LUCY MAUD MONTGOMERY

(1874 – 1942)

THE future saviour of CBC-TV (see **De La Roche, Mazo**, who nearly destroyed it), Montgomery was born in Prince Edward Island, as approximately four billion people on this planet are only too aware of by now. Her mother passed away when she was young, so she was raised by her maternal grandparents after her father chose to move to Prince Albert, Saskatchewan. And who could blame her for staying in P.E.I.? After all, this was long before all the tourists poured in, looking for Anne Shirley, and started to ruin the lovely province, which is only five square kilometres larger than Garth Drabinsky's ego.

After studying at Prince of Wales College in Charlottetown and way out West in Dalhousie University, the young woman looked after her grandmother for the next thirteen years — just the sort of dutiful thing one would expect from the future creator of Anne. During this exciting period in her life, she wrote for various children's magazines in both Canada and the United States, before winning the lottery with her very first book, *Anne of Green Gables*, published in 1908. Interestingly, this most quintessential work about Canada's quintessentially tiny province was first published in Boston, which in retrospect was only proper; most Maritimers end up in Boston sooner or later.

Not unlike Mazo de La Roche's experience with *Jalna*, Montgomery soon found herself trapped by her astonishing success. Anne Shirley became as irresistible as drugs and, as far as Montgomery's writing potential was concerned, just as deadly. If the original *Anne* wasn't enough, it was quickly followed by *Anne of Avonlea* (1909); *Anne of the Island* (1915, and if you ask which island, you're really out of it); *Anne's House of Dreams* (1917); *Anne of Windy Poplars* (1936); *Anne of Ingleside* (1939); and many other volumes in between, every one so sweet that massive use of fluoride in the planet's drinking waters was the only hope of averting an epidemic of tooth decay.

Despite dozens of other books, including a series starring another pubescent girl named Emily, it was Anne who captured the imagination, and, much more important, the book-buying dollars of the entire world. The *Anne* books were translated into more than a dozen languages, made into a hit musical, two films and many TV series, and are even hugely popular in Japan, which makes them the only Canadian product the Land of the Rising Sun will lower itself to purchase.

The title character of *Anne of Green Gables* is today considered the consummate Canadian. This is really quite remarkable, since she is imaginative and spontaneous. She is an orphan when the story begins, and, since she is not American, is never a suspect in her parents' deaths. She is adopted by the elderly brother and sister, Matthew and Marilla, who, being Canadian, are never suspected of incest. As you can see, with a little imagination this *could* have become a rather daring book for its time.

The original novel overflows with wonderful moments, such as Anne's struggle over her hair colour (which spoke to the mothers of the book's readers more than most of their children); her rivalry with Gilbert Blythe, in which Anne easily wins out (see **Atwood, Margaret; Munro, Alice** and most other Canadian women writers); and her decision to give up a scholarship to college in order to stay at home with Marilla after Matthew dies (repelling three generations of feminists, for whom sisterhood is powerful, but a college education is power).

Today Anne Shirley is far larger than Prince Edward Island, which isn't saying very much. But the girl's detractors had their moments, too, in 1974, when the Canadian government put her on a stamp. The chance to lick her behind her back, put a thumb on her face and press down, then throw her into a box, brought additional joy to millions, along with the warming thought that since Canada Post handles the mail in this country, little Anne would sit in a dark container for many days on end before getting crushed by a machine. It's certainly what Gilbert Blythe would have done had Ms. Montgomery possessed a healthy sense of humour.

SUSANNA MOODIE

(1803 – 1885)

SUSANNA Moodie was one of nine irritatingly gifted Strickland children, six of whom wrote and published books and three of whom emigrated to Canada from England, presumably because they couldn't find any work in the States.

Susanna Strickland had already published a book of poems in 1831, at which time she married J. W. Dunbar Moodie, a British army officer who knocked the poetry out of her, thus forcing her to turn to prose. Moodie had been wounded while fighting in Holland in 1827 — whether in a legitimate battle or a bar brawl is lost in time — and so was retired on half pay.

As it happened, half pay was enough to get along on in the young country of Canada, where, in the 1830s, there was nothing much to buy, anyway. Even Toronto housing was remarkably cheap at this time. Calgary's, until 1990, was worthless.

The Moodies, who came with their in-laws, the Traills, soon moved to a grant of 400 acres, north of Peterborough. Who knew then that this would eventually be considered a suburb of Toronto? Not the Moodies. They were poets, not speculators, which is why they had to work for a living.

While in the "backwoods," as they were then affectionately called by new Canadians, the Moodies, or "the honkies," as they were then unaffectionately called by the original Canadians, spent mainly harsh years, clearing a homestead. Today this is accomplished by hiring renovators.

Then came 1837, a date known to few Canadian schoolchildren today, and the rebellion that led to Susanna's husband being recalled to active military duty, or so he told her. This left Susanna Moodie even less free time to pursue her writing career, to the great relief of future students of Canadian literature.

But by 1839, the now Major Moodie, who in retrospect was hardly as major as his gifted wife, was appointed sheriff of Hastings County, so he moved his family to Belleville, Ontario. This prompted his exhausted wife to emit her immortal cry, "I clear trees for half a dozen years and wrestle with bears, and you're now moving us to *Belleville???*"

Still, Belleville allowed Susanna Moodie to spend far more time on writing. As it happened, her poetry was lousy and her fiction was the sort of romantic garbage today published by Torstar's Harlequin Books. Interestingly, the characters of her fictional works were never placed in Canada, probably because Moodie had always hoped for the same thing for herself. (Not to be placed in Canada — get it?)

Where Moodie excelled, however, was in her famous memoirs, *Roughing It in the Bush* (1852), written about the same time as *Walden* and *Moby Dick* but in a slightly different league. (Bush.) Indeed, many Canadian critics marvel, right to this day, that when the United States was putting out world-class literature, Susanna Moodie was writing about cutting down trees and propping up husbands. Students of Canadian literature, on the other hand, are merely mortified.

It was rough all right — and still rough to read today. Happily roughage is good for you, as any mother will confirm, whether Canadian or not.

FROM *ROUGHING IT IN THE BUSH* *(1852)*

NEVER SHALL I FORGET my first arrival at Quebec! I love to recall, even after all these years, every object that awoke in my beating heart such fascination and delight! The funny signs in both English and *anglais*! The charming little French-Canadian families of ten, fifteen and twenty children! (And those were just the priests.) The disarming little restaurants that served only pea soup as main course and Pepsi for beverage! The delightful little stores, where the proprietors tried to speak to us in their silly native language, until finally giving up in frustration and talking to their customers in a proper, civilized tongue.

Canadians, rejoice in your beautiful city! Rejoice and be worthy of her! Who else on earth can boast of a city so filled with intelligent people who can't even speak a word of decent English? Where else on earth, in this modern day and age, is knowledge of French not an asset? Who would not stand up and exclaim, "This is ours! God gave this city to us in all her beauty! And with just a few thousand Protestants, can it not become a beacon to all Mankind?"

Of course, the cholera was a drag, but those are the breaks. Quebec is a beautiful city, and all Canadians, regardless of their ethnic background — Scottish, Irish, English, even, forgive me for saying it, Welsh — can be proud of this city and the glorious country in which it so grandly stands. . . .

(From the conclusion)

Dear Reader! All I have tried to do in this book is to give you a true and faithful picture of one person's life in the backwoods of Canada (forgive the plug for my sister Cathy's book!), and from it you may draw your own conclusions and hew your own wood.

But be warned, darling reader! While this new country of Canada presents many advantages to the industrious working man, it offers *none whatsoever* for the haughty gentleman, unless he has some real connections or Hong Kong money. The former must work hard, put up with lousy food and tolerate hardships that would make a decent Britisher want to move to France, heaven forbid. He will clear the land, get rid of those troublesome Indians and make a fair living, but no more than that. The gentleman, however, would hardly be able to endure such hardship, and would do better to move to the States and have a slave do the work for him. *There's* the life! But to work in a country with five seasons (fall, winter, winter, winter and winter) can lead only to debts and hopeless ruin. And I hear it's even worse out West, on the Prairies. And forget about Calgary.

But if these many stories I have shared with you have kept just one family from selling their homestead back in the Mother Country and choosing to rough it in the bush out in the backwoods of Canada (A double plug, Cathy!), then I shall be very happy, indeed. I went through years of hell in this frozen nightmare — I wouldn't wish it on a Whig — and if you're smart, you'll stay right where you are. Buy my book. Buy all my books, in fact. But to toil and suffer in Canada? I wouldn't wish it on a dog. Have you considered Australia? I gather their aborigines are far less troublesome. Write if you get work.

BRIAN MOORE

(1921 –)

PEOPLE in the know know that the first name is pronounced Bree-an, which can happen to Belfast-born Catholics who don't get shot, and even those who do. And people in the know don't want to know that Moore didn't live and work in Canada long enough to *really* qualify for the title of Canadian writer. (True, Moore *did* labour as a reporter for the Montreal *Gazette* for a few years, but so did Hemingway at the *Toronto Star*, and when's the last time you saw Ernie listed in a university syllabus as a Canadian novelist?)

Still, a number of Moore's finest novels do indeed use Canadian backgrounds, such as *The Luck of Ginger Coffey* (1960), *The Great Victorian Collection* (1975) and *Black Robe* (1986). And they're all damned good, so maybe we *should* try to claim him as our own, even though he had long since moved to the United States to live. But Moore still has his Canadian citizenship, doesn't he? And have there ever been better depictions of women than in *Judith Hearne* and *I Am Mary Dunne*? It can't be denied that we *do* claim **Malcolm Lowry**, do we not? So why *don't* we claim Moore as one of us? And while we're at it, Nobel Prizewinner Saul Bellow spent his toddler years just outside of Montreal, and Oscar Wilde once visited Niagara Falls, Canada, and Charles Dickens once lectured across Canada, and I could swear that I once heard Nobel Prizewinner Isaac Bashevis Singer give a talk in Montreal. . . .

FARLEY MOWAT

(1921 –   )

BORN in Belleville, Ontario, in the Far North of suburban Toronto, Mowat grew up in Saskatoon, then left his schooling at the University of Toronto to serve his country in the Second World War, since at least the Hastings and Prince Edward regiments weren't killing innocent animals but only evil Huns, which doesn't count.

After the war, he spent two years in the Arctic, gathering snow, ice and ideas for future books. Then, after finishing his university degree, he wrote his first book, *People of the Deer* (1952), in which he took to task the treatment of the Inuit by the federal government and by missionaries, although at least the missionaries had a good position. The book was attacked by both the federal government, which wanted only to destroy the Inuit way of life, and the missionaries, who had wanted only to destroy the Inuit religion, but not by the caribou, which were too busy being destroyed by everyone, including the Inuit. Seven years later came the sequel, *The Desperate People*, not as passionate a book as the first, but one that found the Inuit just as desperate, only partly because of Mowat's book.

By the end of the 1980s, Mowat had published nearly three dozen books, which have been translated into over twenty-four languages and published in some forty countries and which all harp on some evil or other, even the killing of harp seals. His most famous animal books, *Never Cry Wolf* (1963) and *A Whale for the Killing* (1972), and his children's fiction, *The Dog Who Wouldn't Be* (1957); *Owls in the Family* (1961); *Lost in the Barrens* (1965); and *The Boat Who Wouldn't Float* (1968); have done much to raise awareness in the next generation of the mistreatment of wolves, whales, dogs, owls, barrens and boats, while murdering millions of trees to print the countless editions of each. Indeed, many critics would put his military memoirs, *And No Birds Sang* (1979) among his children's books, which gives you an idea of how writing for that medium can really soften your brain.

More recently, Mowat has taken on the dying culture of Newfoundland, praising it in *This Rock within the Sea: A Heritage Lost* (1968) and disparaging it in *A Whale for the Killing*, after which his fellow Newfoundlanders attempted to feed him to the last few whales and seals left in the area. They wouldn't bite.

Many critics have challenged the author, pointing out his tendency to exaggerate the facts. Mowat has defended his writing as "subjective nonfiction," which is something he should try with the income tax on his royalty payments. Indeed, while Mowat's books continue to sell worldwide in the hundreds of thousands, he was recently notified by a petition, signed by hundreds of Canadian scholars and historians, that his poetic licence has finally expired.

BHARATI MUKHERJEE

(1940 –)

AN honest-to-God real Indian, but the overseas kind, Ms. Mukherjee was born in Calcutta and studied in England and Switzerland, followed by a stint in Iowa, where she honed her solid writing skills. Then she spent 1966 to 1980 in Canada. The country, as she noted in the introduction to her 1985 collection of stories, *Darkness*, welcomed her in the special way it reserves for "visible minorities": "In Canada, I was frequently taken for a prostitute or shoplifter, frequently assumed to be a domestic."

Today Mukherjee lives in the United States, where she recently made the front page of the *New York Times Book Review* with her brilliant novel *Jasmine*. Still, she *did* live in this country for more than a dozen years, and she *did* place many of her stories in this country, and she *did* marry writer Clark Blaise, the child of French- and English-Canadian parents with whom she wrote both a travel memoir and a nonfiction study of the Air India bombing, and she *has* retained her Canadian citizenship, held proudly next to her new American citizenship. And so, our home and native land has now gained a wonderful new writer we can call our own.

ALICE MUNRO

(1931 –   )

PROBABLY Canada's most wonderful writer, Alice Munro was born in Wingham, Ontario, a farming area near Lake Huron better known today as a place to stay when every hotel near the Stratford Festival is full. She began writing in her early teens, which was not early enough for the many fans of her stories in the *New Yorker*; studied English for two years at the University of Western Ontario in London, which was more than enough; married and moved to Vancouver, where she made three daughters and lost one husband — but not before helping him run a successful family bookstore in Victoria, where the stories she was writing were better than any she sold (in the store).

One of the few authors in history whose collections of short stories usually have titles as brilliant and memorable as the collections themselves — *Lives of Girls and Women* (1971); *Something I've Been Meaning to Tell You* (1974); *Who Do You Think You Are?* (1978); (we'll take a pass on *Dance of the Happy Shades*, 1968) — Munro eventually returned to her original stomping ground by moving to Clinton, Ontario, just a few kilometres/miles physically and psychologically and literally and literarily from where she grew up. More recent collections have been under the slightly less inspired titles of *The Moons of Jupiter* (1982), *The Progress of Love* (1986) and *Friend of My Youth* (1990). The stories, though, keep getting better and better, making most readers come to the decision that **Margaret Atwood**'s and **Mordecai Richler**'s most recent novels didn't really *have* to be more than four hundred pages long. After all, Munro manages to get it all said and done (or not done, which is often the point) in twenty-five pages or less, so why waste all that paper? (Especially what with Atwood's obsession with saving the environment and all.)

Since trying to capture Munro in print is like trying to catch a moonbeam in a jar, to coin a phrase (copyright Richard Rodgers, *The Sound of Music*, 1959, all rights reserved), we shall limit ourselves to the so-called plot of her only "novel," which isn't really a novel at all but a collection of connected short stories, *Lives of Girls and Women*. But, then, Alice Munro isn't really a Canadian novelist at all. She's a collection of connected geniuses through history, from Chekhov to Babel to Fitzgerald to

Paley to Carver, although we're still willing to claim her as our own.

The So-called Plot of Munro's Only So-called Novel

THE BOOK BEGINS with the awakening of the narrator, Del Jordan, to the romance of everyday occurrences and people, including such misfits as Uncle Benny, who reminds you a lot of your in-laws, except that Benny is rendered poetically, while your in-laws should be rendered into chicken fat. Already, only in the first story, Del learns to study the key details of life, which is not only a lovely way to look at the world, but one of the best ways to get her short stories published regularly in the *New Yorker* after she grows up.

For the rest of the thin volume, Del Jordan looks at the various examples of womankind (but not always kind women) whom she runs into in Jubilee, which we have a sneaky suspicion is actually Wingham, but then who knew Wingham before Munro came along? We meet Naomi, Del's closest friend, who chooses to become a wife and a mother like most Jubilee women, even as the reader keeps hoping and praying she won't follow through on this backward resolve. Then there's Marian Sherriff, another young woman of the town, who chooses to kill herself rather than live with an illegitimate child, moving the reader to hope there's a third choice in life, such as writing perfect short stories that get collected into best-selling books and getting the hell out of Wingham, even if only a few miles away.

The really important woman in Del's life ends up being her mother, Ada. This usually comes as a terrifying disappointment to every teenage reader, who knows in his/her heart of hearts that his/her mother is STUPIDDUMBBACKWARDEVILOLDFASHIONEDCRUEL, and that if Alice Munro actually *got along with!* and *learned lots of things from* (!!!) her STUPIDDUMB-BACKWARDEVILOLDFASHIONEDCRUEL mother, then maybe she has the stuff to be a great writer, and maybe the reader doesn't. It's a horrifying realization for most young readers of the book, but not really Munro's fault.

Maybe the key line in the book comes when Del's mother says to her, "There is a change coming in the lives of girls and women. . . . All women have had up till now has been their connection with men. . . ." Which tells us that this book is probably merely feminist. But if it is, then why is it so magnificent? Could this mean . . . ?

Close to the end of the novel/short stories, Del is ready to be baptized into maturity and get on with her real life, which we have to assume means getting married, having daughters, getting rid of Hubby Number One and ending up back where she started, in a one-horse, one-great-fiction-writer, southern Ontario town. And then the book finishes with Del's story becoming a story-within-a-story, as she stops describing her own life and shows how she wrote this book about life in a small southwestern Ontario community where she became a woman. If this sounds dull to you, go back to your Stephen King and Tom Clancy and Danielle Steel. We'll take Alice Munro.

ROBERT MUNSCH

(1945 –)

ROBERT Munsch is one of the most popular and widely read writers for young children in the WHOLE WIDE WORLD!!!!! Born in 1945,

he was a teacher for several years, until HE SUDDENLY TRIPPED OVER THE GREATEST IDEAS FOR BOOKS!!! GREATEST! GREATEST!! **GREATEST!!!** I mean, really HUGE, HUMONGOUS IDEAS!!!

And he sent them away to Annick Books in Toronto, and they LOVED LOVED LOVED THEM, because they were FUNNY and CRAZY and even TASTEFUL now and then.

Some of Munsch's books have sold hundreds of thousands of copies around the world, partly thanks to the wonderful publishing concept of Annikins, TEENY TINY LITTLE WEE PAPERBACK BOOKLETS that sell for only NINETY-NINE CENTS!!!

That's all! Just **NINETY-NINE CENTS!!!!!!** But most of his books are really overpriced, to make up for the Annikins.

Anyway, some of his books are REEEEEEALLY GRRRRRREAT, and some are not so great, but that's okay, too, because when you consider the dreck on TV, Munsch is SHHHHHHHHAKESPEARE!!

What's great about Munsch is that his books are short,

and funny, and silly, and even kinda dirty, like the one about a kid who goes for a ride with his parents and then HAS TO GO!!!!! You know — like PEEEEE! That's a really good one. And the one about the kid who was adopted by a giant was REALLY GREAT, 'cause it makes adopted kids feel better, and stuff like that. And it's just WONDERFUL that Robert Munsch has lots of tapes and records of him reading, because he reads everything REEEEEEAAALLY FUNNY, and AWWWWWWFULLY SILLLLLY, and that's great, because he's almost as much fun as watching TV or playing Nintendo. Almost.

Anyway, Munsch wrote a book a few years ago called *Love You Forever* that was kinda STRANGE and WEEEEIIIIRRRRD 'cause it made kids giggle and made their parents cry, which got everyone confused, because it was about a mummy who takes care of her little boy and then the kid grows up to be a man and he has to take care of his mummy, who is now OOOOOOOOLLLLLD. I don't see why all the parents cry over that, when it's really kind of funny. Maybe it's because Mummy and Daddy know there's not a snowball's chance in HELLLLLL that their kids will ever take care of them like the little boy in the book who grows up to be a man. Anyway, that book sold hundreds of thousands of copies, because kids love to laugh and parents love to cry, and now you know the difference between the generations if you didn't know already. And it sold well in the UNITED STATES, TOOOOOOOOO!!!

Munsch is fun and really great because he has lots of pictures and easy words and he YELLS a lot, both on the page and on his tapes. He makes me laugh, just like the six-and-a-half hours of TV that I get to watch every night.

MUNSCH IS THE GREATEST!!!!!!!!

SUSAN MUSGRAVE

(1951 –)

THE jackrabbit's prole.

PETER C. NEWMAN

(1929 –)

THE man who made power interesting in Canada and gave business a good name, or at least a good market in the bookstores, Peter C. (for Cash) Newman was born in Vienna, but came to Canada in 1940 on a wartime scholarship. When he first arrived, he studied at Upper Canada College, where he was so grateful to have escaped Hitler, he promised all his wealthy fellow students that he would make them famous. After earning his B.A. and M.B.A. at the University of Toronto, he began a career in magazines, newspapers and books that can be matched only by **Pierre Berton**'s.

In fact, there are theories, not yet disproven, that Peter C. Newman really *is* Pierre Berton. (Be honest. Have you *ever* seen the two of them in a room together?) Here is the proof:

Berton wrote for the University of British Columbia's undergraduate newspaper, *The Ubyssey*; Newman did the same for the University of Toronto's *Varsity*.

Berton became city editor of the Vancouver *News-Herald* and later the *Sun*; Newman joined *The Financial Post*.

Maclean's recruited Berton and moved him to Toronto in 1947; Newman joined the same magazine ten years later. (But, once again, *they were never seen together*! *Ever*.) True, both worked for the *Toronto Star* for several years, and in

various capacities, which only underlines the stunning coincidences.

Berton wrote his first book, *The Royal Family* (1954), from a series of articles that first appeared in *Maclean's*; Newman's first book, *Flame of Power* (1959), was based on his journalistic experience at *The Financial Post* and *Maclean's*.

Berton became a TV star ("My Country," "The Great Debate," etc.); Newman became a TV star ("The Tenth Decade," "Hail and Farewell," etc.).

Furthermore — and here's where it gets frightening, dear reader — Berton was raised in Victoria and has been firmly ensconced in Toronto since the late 1940s; Newman, who lived in Toronto for forty years, purportedly moved to Victoria in the 1980s.

Both men have had countless best-sellers, often appearing on best-seller lists at the same time! And in most of their books, they have both been "popular historians." *And they have never been photographed together!!!*

True, Newman alone has made it hard not to think of Canadian politicians, hard not to think of Canadian businessmen and hard not to think of The Bay. But he's made it hard to read about them — an intriguing fact because his books still sell in the hundreds of thousands. Here's a brief example of why:

MOTHER TERESA (FROM *THE CANADIAN ESTABLISHMENT*, 1975).

MOTHER TERESA MAKES AN UNLIKELY Canadian businessman: first, she is not a Canadian; second, she is not a man; and third, and probably the most important, she knows zip about business. She even gives things away, helping others to health care and food, without even *attempting* to make a huge profit from it. Calcutta is a long way from Toronto, or even Edmonton, and Terry's actions have clearly shown it. Her penny stock has tumbled on the VSE, and in the minds of everyone who knows her, except those who are actually impressed by her bleeding-heart do-goodism, which includes few, if any, of those who lunch daily at Winston's Restaurant, the place where food really counts (and costs), in the heart of Toronto's business district. And where new clothing is a must.

Terry's Catholicism would never be held against her in Canada — it sure didn't hurt Paul Desmarais — but the way she ignores the usual rules of greed and money-lust makes her an unimpressive member of the Canadian Establishment. Her lack of a home life can also be ignored, including her lack of a husband, for this, too, is not unknown in Canada, since many a top businessman will dump a spouse on the way to the top. But Terry's liberal sensibilities have crushed her chances for favours from anyone but the pinkest MPs in Ottawa, which makes me wonder why I have even included her in this book. Still, with an indoor swimming pool, a five-million-dollar home on Toronto's Bridle Path, a lover or two and a better accountant, Terry might have a greater chance of cracking this country's higher echelons of power. But giving away food, clothes and health care reeks of the kind of (forgive the obscenity) *socialism* that strikes fear and loathing into the hearts of even the most generous Canadian businessmen. And "Big Mama" Terry most certainly should have known that by now.

bp NICHOL

(1944 – 1988)

mustbeheardtobebelieved

MUST be HEARRRRRRRRD TO BE
BELIEEEEEEEEVED

MUST

BE

HEAR(D)

2-B

BE
L
E
A
F
E
D

!!!!!

Eric Nicol

(1919 –)

NOT much of a playwright, but one helluva funny author of books about Canada, sports and more. That great non-Canadian W. C. Fields was once asked his opinion about fellow comedian Charlie Chaplin, and he replied, "That man is the greatest ballet dancer of all time, and if I ever meet him, I'll break both his legs." The author of this book plans to do the same to Eric Nicol's pen/typewriter/computer.

Alden Nowlan

(1933 – 1983)

ONE of the bards, as well as beards, of the Maritimes, Alden Nowlan was so regional the barnacles were still on him at the time of his untimely death. After being born in Stanley, Nova Scotia, which was already a guarantee of childhood poverty and despair, he left school in his early teens, having graduated from grade four without honours. A self-educated man, he cut pulp long before he wrote it, served as a nightwatchman in a sawmill and was even a highwayman in that he worked for the Nova Scotia Department of Highways. He also served as a newspaperman, managed a country music band, wrote short stories, wrote poems and became a respected writer across Canada, even though he had received an Honorary Doctor of Laws from the University of New Brunswick and had written several plays. For all the simple quality of his language and the directness of his themes, even his harshest critics cannot deny that the titles of some of his collections of poetry are among the best ever written by anyone, Canadian or otherwise, grade five dropout or Ph.D. in math, including: *A Darkness in the Earth* (1959), *Things Which Are* (1962), *The Mysterious Naked Man* (1969), *Playing the Jesus Game* (1970), *I'm a Stranger Here Myself* (1974) and *I Might Not Tell Everybody This* (1982). The nice thing is, in the case of his last collection, he tried to.

MICHAEL ONDAATJE

(1943 –)

INDISPUTABLY the best Ceylonese poet in the history of Canada, Ondaatje had a most interesting youth, as you should know already from having read his fascinating autobiographical work, *Running in the Family* (1982). He's not the most successful Ceylonese businessman in the history of Canada, however; that honour is held by his brother, Christopher, who did for stocks what Michael did for poetry. After coming to Canada in 1962, the writer began to publish his poems in 1967 with *The Dainty Monsters*, which he has continued to create with his violent, powerful, exotic, terrifying writing ever since.

Ondaatje's poetry and novels have covered such all-Canadian topics as women who have been shipwrecked off the coast of Australia, the life of the famed American outlaw Billy the Kid, drunken jazz musicians, spiders, dragons, gorillas and even such absurd concepts as Toronto. But what can you expect from a man whose native country changed its name to Sri Lanka after the Ondaatje family left?

ANN ONYMOUS

THIS Greek-Scot author was one of the most prolific in early Canada, writing many tens of thousands of poems, published over a century and a half. The one included here is from the middle of the eighteenth century, when Lord Cornwallis arrived in Nova Scotia with some 2,500 men and women. Their goal was to settle the young town of Halifax. A thrilling side effect was ballads such as the following, which was first published back in England in 1750.

A BALLAD OF NOVA SCOTIA

Let's split to New Scotland, where cool cash is found
In the happiest country that e'er did come 'round;
It blesses its cit'zens, both minor and grand,
With a house for ten pounds and five more for the land.
    Derry down, [down, down, derry down].

There's wood and there's water, an' big game ta kill,
And a few Injun tribes that'r over the hill;
Good feed for our cattle, good land for our shovels,
Which sure beats Ol' Englund, where we all lived in hovels.
    Injun down [down, down, Injun down, etc.]

No landlords ta push us around anymore!
Now *we'll* be the landlords, with profits galore!

Who cares for the Micmac? Who bleeds for the Cree?
It's 'bout time that we became "Generation — Me!"
Micmac down [Micmac paddywhack, give 'em just a bone, etc.]

There are no taxes here, to drive us all nits
Only new fruits to eat, since the old was the pits.
We are free men again! Our wrongs put to right!
If the Injuns would join us, they'll have ta be white.
Injuns down [Scots up, up, Injuns down, down, way down, etc.]

P. K. PAGE

(1916 –)

BORN in England; came to Canada as a toddler (to Red Deer, Alberta, where there was nothing to do but toddle); never went to university (which helps explain why her poetry is so very good); worked as a scriptwriter for the National Film Board (which shouldn't be held against anybody — look how Germany and Japan are both trading partners of ours today); travelled with her ambassador husband to Australia, Brazil and Mexico, where she became an accomplished painter; wrote quality poems ranging from *As Ten As Twenty* (1946) through *Cry Ararat! Poems New and Selected* (1974) and beyond. The fact that she is not studied in depth in every high school and university English course in Canada says more about this country than about her art, since the latter is possibly too good for the former.

E. J. PRATT

(1882 – 1964)

BORN in a Newfoundland village on Conception Bay, which already suggested fruitfulness, Edwin John Pratt grew up in various coastal communities and was trained to follow his father into the Methodist ministry. He even preached on the island as a young man, long before being a religious leader in Newfoundland had become a kind of Newfie joke of its own.

In 1907, however, the young Pratt moved to Toronto and enrolled at Victoria College of the University of Toronto, where he got his B.A., M.A. and Ph.D., making him capable of doing nothing but teaching for the rest of his life. Indeed, he joined the faculty of English in 1920, where he remained for a third of a century, instructing students, writing poems, sinking the *Titanic*, hunting whales, getting fish and cats drunk, torturing Jesuit priests, refighting World War II and building the railroad. Yet, some people still wonder why professors fight for tenure.

From his *Newfoundland Verse* (1923) to his *Towards the Last Spike* (1952), Pratt flooded Canada's bookstores, universities, schools and libraries with his poems, many of them displaying the fluidity and power of skreech, the favourite soft drink of his native province.

AL PURDY

(1918 –)

BORN in Woller, Ontario, a village near Trenton, which is also somewhere in that province, Purdy has claimed being "of degenerate Loyalist stock" — and who am I to argue? He left school at sixteen, something I recommend to most of my readers, and began to wander across the country, and eventually around the entire world, several times. He rode the freight trains out to Vancouver in 1937, then turned around and hopped an eastbound train the very day of his arrival, probably because someone told him about the provincial politics of British Columbia.

After marrying, fathering a son and serving in the RCAF on the Skeena River in northern B.C., where he encountered few of the enemy, aside from the many fellow soldiers who didn't wish to hear him read his poetry, Purdy eventually paid to have 500 copies of his first book of poetry, *The Enchanted Echo*, published for him. A warehouse worker purportedly destroyed nearly three-quarters of the edition, which only goes to prove that everyone's a critic.

For many years, Purdy worked in a mattress factory in Vancouver (which is surprising, because so few of his poems are restful), then moved to Montreal in 1956, where he met such (then) promising poets as **Louis Dudek** and **Irving Layton**. Eventually he worked for another mattress company in Montreal, proving that some of his talent was catching on nearly from coast to coast.

Millions of poems have followed, collected in such volumes as *Poems for All the Annettes* (1962), *The Cariboo Horses* (1965), which won a Governor General's Award, *Being Alive* (1978) and other gatherings too numerous to mention, since there are a limited number of pages allotted to the book you're now reading. Since he has frequently written about hockey, the following image might be apt: Al Purdy is forever shooting, missing, slashing, slapping, tripping, offside and frequently onside, as quick to write —

or read — a poem as a puck being dropped. If you are ever stopped on a street corner and a balding, smiling, long-faced man yells out, "You wanna hear a poem?" it's probably Purdy.

Say yes.

James Reaney

(1926 –)

Both a poet and a playwright, which can be a pretty deadly combination (see T. S. Eliot, Christopher Fry and lots of other poet/playwrights whose efforts aren't really worth seeing on the stage, although on the page, maybe), James Reaney was born on a farm near Stratford, Ontario, more than a quarter century before the area went Renaissance. He attended the University of Toronto, which was one of the few ways of escaping the family farm in those days (today bankruptcy is the primary fashion), earned an M.A., taught in Manitoba for several years and then returned to U. of T. to complete his Ph.D., since he never would have managed to escape Manitoba without one. (His thesis was on the influence of Spenser on Yeats, suggesting that Reaney would be a different kind of Canadian writer, since those guys are rarely studied in our schools.)

Reaney's books of poetry were widely acclaimed by the many hundreds of Canadians who follow this country's poetry scene. *The Red Heart* (1940), his very first collection, won the Governor General's Award; he would win it twice more with *A Suit of Nettles* (1958) and *Twelve Letters to a Small Town* and *The Killdeer and Other Plays*

(1962). This is known in Canadian literary lingo as "a hat trick," something that Saskatchewan native Gordie Howe and Quebec native Maurice Richard had made famous much earlier.

Reaney's plays have earned him even greater kudos, if not royalties, ranging from the highly poetic *Listen to the Wind* (1966) and *Colours in the Dark* (1967), to a highly theatrical study of the famous Donnelly family in an unholy trilogy of works. *The Donnellys, Part I*, also known as *Sticks and Stones*, which also hurt them, introduces that wild group of Irish Catholics who gained great fame (if not long life) by being slaughtered by their neighbours just outside London, Ontario, in 1880. This was seen as vulgar and unnecessary in southwestern Ontario at the time. Most immigrants were allowed to just move peacefully to Toronto, where they would all die on Sundays from Nothingtodo, a virtual epidemic in that city into the late 1950s.

Like all soon-to-be-murdered people, the Donnellys are highly sympathetic and noble, even though they are labelled as "troublemakers" and "blackfeet" and "barn burners," the last of which should really have been a badge of honour, since the Mounties would later do it to great acclaim. The second play, *The St. Nicholas Hotel*, looks back on how some of the Donnellys began a stagecoach line in competition with their neighbours. This, of course, enraged the good Protestant hierarchy, since competition had not been legal in Ontario since the province's earliest beginnings. In the final installment, *Handcuffs*, the Donnellys are all murdered, their killers are all acquitted and everyone lives happily ever after. It's sort of like the history of the Canadian Indian (see **Kinsella, W. P.; Ryga, George; Wiebe, Rudy**; and a few other whites).

MAJOR JOHN RICHARDSON

(1796 – 1852)

UNTIL modern times, Richardson was Canada's only major writer, although most would argue that the only thing major about him was his military title. Born in Queenston, on the Niagara frontier, John Richardson knew the falls even before they were a tourist attraction. But that's water over the dam now. One would have hoped that, as the eldest son of a surgeon, he would have the understanding to cut down his own writing. But to no avail. Most of his books go on like a politician during Question Period, often to many hundreds of pages.

Richardson spent his childhood at Amherstburg, on the Canadian border, not far from where Brock and Tecumseh later fought in the War of 1812. The rich historical setting provided him with far too much background ever to be a good novelist. As a young soldier, he was actually captured by the Americans, although they had the good sense not to be captivated by his later writings. Knowing Pontiac even before he was a car would provide further grist for the future author's literary mill.

Unlike the members of most armies of this century, prisoners of war were actually allowed to live, in the early nineteenth century, which meant that Richardson was released from captivity in 1814. Still unaware that his pen would be more financially lucrative than his sword, the youth went off to England and began a long career as a soldier, living the soldier's life: looting, raping and rampaging across Barbados, Spain, Paris and, daringly, London, as well. His first novel, *Ecarte*, was published in England in 1829, even though it had a French name and described what the critics have called "his gay life as a British officer in Paris." In spite of Richardson's never having attended an English boarding school, he was still capable of having a gay life. And he married twice yet.

Then, in 1832, his most famous novel, the historical romance *Wacousta*, was published. It came out the same year Sir Walter Scott died, but not a single critic on either side of the Atlantic has ever suggested that the soul of the author of *Ivanhoe* leapt into the body of the Canadian. The book was a fabulous best-seller and was reprinted many times, proving that the popularity of a work does not reflect its quality.

In 1838, Richardson, now a major, returned to his homeland to report for the London *Times* on the famous Canadian rebellion of the previous year. But the Brits were no more interested in it than the Canadians were. He now proceeded to turn out book after book after book, none of them worth mentioning, except that most were printed in his own literary weekly, which he published in Brockville, Ontario, in the early 1840s. The idea of Brockville being a hotbed of literary arts is a source of humour to Canadian scholars to this very day.

Finally Richardson made it, in that he moved to the States. Jobs were few and far between in Hollywood, so he spent all his time in New York State, turning out penny versions of his many books, thus guaranteeing himself at least a half-dozen mediocre doctoral theses on his life and work. Sadly, the royalties on one-cent novels were surprisingly low, which led to his starving to death. (Back home he would have frozen first.) Although he died in 1852, no one knows where he is buried. Not that there is a long lineup of fans wanting to locate his gravesite. Even in the middle of the last century, Canadian writers found anonymity would hound them everywhere, even after death.

Because *Wacousta* is endless and its story highly complex, I have chosen merely to share the plot with you. If this assists you in never having to read the entire book, you have only me to thank.

The plot of *Wacousta, or the Prophecy*, published in three volumes (!), unfolds largely through flashbacks. The scene is Fort Detroit, where Pontiac struggles against British power, while Chevy and Buick hover in the wings, fearful of the eastern attack of Toyota, Nissan and Honda.

Sadly, the reader has to struggle through some one thousand pages before realizing the truth about several British army officers, Charles De Haldimar and Sir Reginald Morton, who have been poaching on the Scottish Highlands following their victory over the Jacobite rebels in the mid-1700s. I hope you've been taking notes.

Anyway, Reggie has fallen head over boots in love with Clara Beverley, a young woman of the female persuasion. But his best friend, Chuck, wins her love through betraying Reggie, then getting him kicked out of the army in shame. Imagine if they had been enemies.

Reggie Morton responds in the only way a romantic hero in the nineteenth-century novel could have responded: he passes himself off as the Indian Wacousta, a sort of white Tonto to Pontiac's Kemo sabe.

Twenty years, and twenty hours of reading, pass. Chuck De Haldimar has taken over the command of Detroit, which wasn't much nicer back then than it is today. And you can guess what happens. Wacousta plots revenge against his former best friend, succeeding in killing Chuck, one of his sons, and his daughter. Nowadays any visit to Detroit can achieve the same result, but without all the vengeance stuff.

With its absurd story, its endless expositions, its tedious love scenes and its silly dialogue, the only surprise is why CBC-TV has not turned *Wacousta* into a miniseries before now. But wait, wait. Sir Reginald Morton did, and look how he got what he wanted.

MORDECAI RICHLER

(1931 – until a member of the Montreal Jewish community finally murders him)

MOR-DE-KAI *Ritch*-ler, or Mor-de-*chii Rish*-ler, or Mor-de-*chchchchyyy Rich-liar*, depending on your ethnic background, the one-time *enfant terrible* of Canadian literature, has grown into a terrible infant, and in less than four decades.

Richler was born in Montreal. The year was 1931, a time when things were looking really bad for his coreligionists over in Europe. Young Mordecai, always sensitive to the world around him, made a vow that he would work to make things look really bad for his coreligionists in Canada. Why should they be left out? he thought.

It was not an easy time to be a Jew, nor an easy place to be a Jew. Montreal, in the 1930s, was a place of two solitudes: white Anglo-Saxon Protestants, who were busy bleeding Quebec of all its land and money, and white

French-speaking Catholics, who *wanted* to bleed Quebec of all its land and money, but couldn't wrestle the power away from *les maudits anglais*. Actually, there was a third solitude, whom Richler would turn into art over the 1950s, 1960s, 1970s and 1980s: the white, but non-Anglo-Saxon-Protestant and non-French-speaking-Catholic *Jews*, who saw all this great bleeding of Quebec land and money around them and wanted to try it, too, but were worried sick that the WASPs and Québécois would get angry at them (*les maudits juifs*) for desiring to do something as terrible as that.

Anyway, where were we? Oh, yes. So Mordecai Richler, neither of whose names sounds right in either of our two official languages, grew up the son of a junk dealer and a loving mother. The influence of both his parents was great: in honour of his father, he wrote junk for several years; in honour of his mother, who was the daughter of a rabbi, he made fun of Jewish women and rabbis for several more years. Ridiculing your own people isn't particular to the Jews, of course. Do recall that many of the works of James Joyce are still banned in his beloved Ireland. The big difference is, when writing is judged to be critical in *most* countries, the works are banned and/or the author imprisoned. In Canada, the works are simply ignored and the author either starves to death or moves elsewhere.

After several years of private religious schooling, where Richler got enough goods on his fellow Jews to ridicule them for his first dozen novels, he attended the now famous Baron Byng High School, which he labelled "Fletcher's Field" in *The Apprenticeship of Duddy Kravitz*. To this day, the descendants of Baron Byng thank their lucky stars that Richler chose to change the name of the school.

The teachers at the school were predominantly Anglo-

Saxon Protestants, and the students at the school were predominantly of East European Jewish descent, which made for more sparks than at an arsonists' convention. The only happy people in the area were the French-speaking Catholics, who hoped against hope that the others would kill one another off. The descriptions of Baron Byng/Fletcher's Field seem almost quaint today, since the teachers and students actually spoke a strange, foreign language called "English," which has since fallen into disfavour in the province of Quebec.

Richler did poorly in high school, mainly because he used to stagger around the halls of the institution, mumbling the words of his revered grandfather, "A man without a best-selling novel is a nobody." Tragically, his low grades meant that he could not get into McGill University and could only be accepted by Sir George Williams College. The future novelist later called Sir George Williams "a loser's finishing school," which is such a good line I couldn't improve on it. Fortunately most of his novels make my work a lot easier.

Always out to hurt his parents, as well as to shock the Anglo-Saxon and French-Catholic majority, who were anxious to hate the Jews for being rich (and here was Richler, the poor son of a junk dealer) and for being so damned smart (and here was Richler, unable to get into McGill), Richler did not even graduate from Sir George Williams College. Now, fortunately, the Anglo-Saxon and French-Catholic majority was able to mock this little Jew, who wasn't even bright enough to get into McGill, much less graduate from Sir George Williams College. As most ethnic groups can tell you even today, it's not easy to make it in Canada.

Which is why Richler headed off to France in 1951 after cashing in his life insurance policy. In retrospect, terminating the policy was an extremely risky thing to do, since soon after his first few books were published in Canada, large numbers of the Montreal Jewish community wanted to kill him.

Why Paris? you ask. Had not Richler had enough French shoved down his throat back in Montreal? Not at all. The Québécois didn't start shoving French down Anglo throats until the Reign of Terror of Trudeau. No, it was because Paris was *the* place to escape to when you weren't recognized at home.

Paris! Where Ernest Hemingway had gone to escape the pettiness of the Toronto of the 1920s! Paris! Where F. Scott Fitzgerald had gone to escape the philistinism of the United States! Paris! Where T. S. Eliot had gone to escape the boredom of the U.S. and England! How could Paris *not* welcome Mordecai Richler of Canada? (The fact that Hemingway, Fitzgerald and Eliot all disliked Jews didn't bother Richler. He wasn't too fond of the Jews, either.)

The young Canadian expatriate starved for a while, visiting Spain and England with his spare poverty. In the latter country, at least, Richler spoke the language fairly well. Not so in his first book, *The Acrobats*, which reads like Ernest Hemingway with a hangover. There was one major difference, however. Ernest Hemingway had a hangover most of the time and he still wrote well, until he started imitating Ernest Hemingway. Richler imitated Hemingway imitating Hemingway, and it was awful.

Naturally, the book was praised in London and translated into five languages. Canadian critics hated it, though, which gave Richler more reasons to stay away from his homeland. In 1954 he settled in London. Within a year, the ex-Montrealer was forced to do what all decent writers must do: write about what they know, which in Richler's case was the Jewish community of Montreal. The book was entitled *Son of a Smaller Hero*, although it was soon realized that its proper name should have been *Son of a Smaller Duddy*. Then came *A Choice of Duddies* (1957), and possibly his most famous, influential work, *The Apprenticeship of Duddy Kravitz*, in 1959 — well, influential on the career of Mordecai Richler, at least.

A widening circle of wildly different works followed: *The Incomparable Duddy* (1963), *Duddysure* (1968), *St. Urbain's Duddy* (1971), *Duddy Then and Now* (1980) and *Duddy Gursky Was Here* (1989). He also published two children's books, *Duddy Two-Two, Kravitz Four* (1976) and *Duddy Two-Two and the Duddysaur* (1987). No one seems to know why Richler took so long between his last few novels; it is clear that he has it in him.

To be fair (which Richler has rarely been to Canada or his fellow Jews) the author has spent much of the past three decades avoiding the difficulty and seriousness of writing novels by knocking off those little things that *really* pay well: magazine articles by the hundreds, on subjects as wide-ranging as baseball, Canada, baseball in Canada, Canadian baseball and many more. He also was on the board of the Book of the Month Club for many years, allowing him to pass judgment on his betters, and occasionally sneak his own novels in as Alternate Choices.

True, Richler has often turned out books of essays, as well, such as *The Street* (about Montreal), *Hunting Tigers under Glass* (mainly about Montreal), *Home Sweet Home* (often about Montreal) and an anthology of modern humour. The latter had surprisingly few entries about Montreal, since, as any Montrealer will tell you, that great, impoverished city is no laughing matter.

And so, Mordecai Richler lived for nearly twenty years in the Mother Country of England, since, as the old saying goes, "A man without a homeland is a nobody." While in

London, he tossed off numerous film scripts, which were just as quickly tossed off by the movie critics, before he finally returned to his beloved Montreal, where he had managed to alienate several million white Anglo-Saxon Protestants, French Canadians and the few Jews who hadn't already moved to Toronto due to French-English tensions. Richler vowed to keep writing about the city's dwindling Jewish community. This is known, in an old French expression, as "adding insult to injury."

Still, turning a new novel out every decade or so on subjects ranging from the Jews of Montreal to the Montreal Jewish community has led to a worldwide following for Canada's homegrown boy. (Even though he lost his job at the Book of the Month Club.) There was no longer any need to escape to Spain or to England. Now Richler could afford to sit back, relax, keep dashing off magazine articles for American periodicals on how quaint and silly Canadians are and keep praying that his homes in Montreal and the Eastern Townships would increase in value as much as the homes of his fellow writers in Toronto.

Richler, now approaching sixty, if no longer writing like sixty (even in kilometres), might be most proud of one glorious episode in his career, for which he can claim total credit: his choosing Richard Dreyfuss to star in the movie version of *The Apprenticeship of Duddy Kravitz* helped make that American actor's career. As both Dreyfuss and Richler would agree, "A man without a hundred grand is a nobody."

Today, at the beginning of the 1990s, Mordecai Richler is accepted at last, and even loved, by everybody in Canada except the people on whose lives and backs he had built his literary career: the Montreal Jewish community.

Just like Duddy Kravitz, at the end of that novel. This is known, in an old Yiddish expression, as "life imitating art."

FROM *THE APPRENTICESHIP OF DUDDY KRAVITZ*

WHAT *NARISHKEIT*!" DUDDY SAID, pulling open the refrigerator. "*Oy*, such *chazer-fleisch* in here," he *kvetched*, slamming the door, but not before taking out some *schmaltz* and spreading it all over the *shiksa*'s lovely, non-Jewish, and therefore perfect, body.

"Isn't this a bit kinky?" Yvette giggled in that charming Frenchy accent of hers.

"It makes you smell more like a *yiddele*," said Duddy with a grin, embracing her while refusing to *kibitz*. "You know, if it weren't for that *fershtunkene goniff*, I might have not have been stuck with that *shlock* deal. You got any *shekels*?"

"*Qu'est-ce que c'est*?" Yvette queried.

"Look, I hate to be a *schnorrer*," explained the lad, "but I got to buy *Zeyda* something before he splits to *shul* for the afternoon *dovening*."

"*Pardon*?" asked Yvette once more, her lack of *menschlichkeit* showing in the *chutzpah* she displayed by not understanding the young *schlemiel*.

"*Gey geharget!*" screamed Duddy, suddenly in a rage. "All I get from you is *bubkas* and the occasional *kregel*. You're probably a *shicker* as well as a *shiksa*! If you didn't smell so sweetly of *schmaltz*, I'd throw you out on your *tuchos*. When are you stupid dumb *goyim* gonna learn to talk the official language of Quebec?"

Oy vay, thought Yvette, as the *schmaltz* on her perfect, *shiksa* body made her slide off the bed and onto the hard floor of the apartment, her sweet *tuchos* slapping against the ground *oytzkashpreit*. "For such a *furshlugginer golem* I put out?" she blurted from her perfectly shaped, *chazer*-eating lips.

Duddy broke into a wide, toothy smile. "*Now* you're talking," he said with a laugh. "You see? You see?"

"A *mensch* without *parnossa* is *effes*," Yvette managed to say, looking up from the floor at her *Yiddishe pusherke* anti-hero.

"You've got it! I think you've got it!" shrieked Duddy, as he danced her around the room. *"Mazel tov!"*

A shiksa *without a* lingua yiddisha *ain't* effes, *either*, Yvette thought, vowing to get rid of the *chazer-fleisch*, keep *kosher* for her little *shaneh punim*, enter a *Yeshiva* for *balalat tshuva*, and shave her *keppel* and wear a *shaytel*, just like her little *yingele* would want.

When am I gonna dump this broad and get married to a nice Jewish girl from Westmount? thought Duddy, his face a mask radiating the sweetness of a fresh, toasted bagel with cream cheese and Nova Scotia lox across the top. "Hey, Yvette, why don't we hop across rue Ste. Famille for some pea soup, frogs' legs and a Pepsi?"

"Racist *chazer*," Yvette cried, weeping and digging her nails into his scrawny, Dreyfussian *punim*.

They both fell to the ground in a simultaneous epileptic fit, as Virgil walked into the apartment, suddenly deeply moved by the profound empathy of his two good friends.

"Gevalt!" Virgil cried out. *"A be gezunt!"*

"Shaneh dank," said Duddy, as he got up from the floor. Such a little *pusherke* like him wasn't the type to have a grand mal, which was a French term, anyway, the stupid dumb *goyim*. Duddy smiled. Maybe the dumb *sheygitz* truck driver *was* learning something about life, after all, the *chazer-fresser*.

"I see that you've been *larnen* your *Haftorah* from me," giggled Duddy Richlerianly. "You're starting to talk like a real *Quebecnik*."

"Actually, it's because I read *Mad* magazine every month," said Virgil.

"*Fershtunkene* New York *Yiddin*," hissed Duddy angrily. "What the *gehenna* do they *farshtay*, anyway? *They've* never gone to Protestant schools, lived beneath the shadow of un *groyse goyishekop* cross and read *Maria Chapdelaine*. What the *dreck* do *they* know about Judaism?"

SIR CHARLES G. D. ROBERTS

(1860 – 1943)

BORN in the marshes north of Fredericton, Roberts grew up in the parsonage of his Anglican clergyman father in Sackville, a place even less interesting than Fredericton. His mother could trace her lineage back to relatives of Ralph Waldo Emerson, which was her only claim to fame. Women were forced to do things like that in the nineteenth century in order to make conversation.

Roberts' ancestors included teachers of Greek and Latin, however, which was no claim to fame whatsoever. In fact, Roberts' first cousin was **Bliss Carman**, who was well known for bragging that his family was related to Ralph Waldo Emerson and had Greek and Latin teachers in it, but this didn't work for *that* Canadian poet, either.

As a teenager, little Charles moved with his family back to Fredericton, showing just how little Canadians got around in the last quarter of the nineteenth century. Of course, that was before we had so many trains criss-crossing the country. Actually, it was sort of like today.

The headmaster of the school attended by Charles G. D. Roberts was a brilliant scholar who turned the young man, as well as his Blissful cousin, on to Homer, Virgil, Horace, Keats, Shelley, Tennyson, Browning and Arnold. Roberts' father, as a clergyman, was horrified that his son was being turned on by all these older men, but he said and did nothing, sort of like Newfoundland religious leaders in our own time.

Roberts attended the University of New Brunswick in the late 1870s, where he grew to love Greek and Latin. Clearly this was in the family blood, sort of like diabetes. Most of the student's time, however, was spent writing poems, to the consternation of his friends and the tedium of his readers.

In 1880, a year that will live in infamy because of it, Roberts published his first book, *Orion and Other Poems.* He was twenty, an age when most young men in Canada would someday be flipping burgers or watching TV. (To be fair, many young people today remain thrilled and inspired by Homer, especially hit by Freddy McGriff; and love Shelley, both parts of Ms. Winters' autobiography; and get a great kick out of Arnold, especially Schwarzenegger's more violent flicks.)

At this same tender age, Roberts became headmaster of a school where the children, in an act of strength and good taste rarely witnessed in the previous century, adamantly refused to have his poetry taught in their classes. Then Roberts got married to a young woman who immediately became known affectionately as "Mrs. Roberts." Life was like that for Canadian women in the 1880s. (And the 1980s, too, when I last checked.)

Roberts took his M.A. degree at the University of New Brunswick before anyone noticed, or even insisted that he give it back, and he moved on to become the headmaster of another school, this one in Fredericton. Some scholars have concluded that he left the earlier school so abruptly because his deep love for Virgil, Horace, Shelley and Arnold had been discovered. Let no one say that the past century was dull, even in the Maritimes. Christian brothers take note, if not encouragement.

When a new journal was being planned in Toronto in 1883, Roberts was promptly invited to come and edit the magazine. He had heard a lot about Toronto that attracted him: its many thousands of white, Anglo-Saxon Protestants; its spotless, crime-free streets; its spotless, people-free streets; its lack of pubs; its three and four banks on every major corner; but most of all, its lack of idiotic castles, domed stadiums, ugly towers and money-grubbing businessmen. And he liked what he saw, until he discovered that it cost *hundreds of dollars* to build or purchase a new house in the city. Were its citizens out of their minds?

Anyway, Roberts soon quit his job because he could not get along with his editor, the famous Goldwin Smith. It appeared that Smith had no taste in poetry, as shown by his lack of desire to publish Roberts' verse; he was clearly a philistine.

Roberts wrote for various magazines until 1885, when a college in Nova Scotia appointed him to its faculty of French and English many decades before Canada became officially bilingual. Later the brilliant teacher became a professor of English and economics, many decades before English stopped being used in the Maritimes and almost a full century before Pierre Trudeau put an end to the use of economics in the entire country.

Roberts worked as a professor for a full decade, writing several books and struggling valiantly to get his students to use them in his classes. Even declaring them mandatory was to no avail. Back then, like today, students were revolting.

Roberts went free-lance once more in the mid-1890s,

the same year Chekhov was writing his magnificent short stories and plays in Russia; the same year Henrik Ibsen was changing drama forever in Norway; the same year Oscar Wilde in England and Mark Twain in the United States were penning some of the most hilarious works in history. Other than writing in the same year, there was absolutely nothing that could possibly connect the Canadian with these men. Canada is like that. (Although, to be fair, Oscar Wilde *also* passionately loved Virgil, Horace, Shelley and Arnold. As well as Alfred, Pierre, Jean, Maximilian, Jacques and so many others.)

In 1897, Roberts moved to New York with his cousin Bliss. There he served as an assistant editor of a minor magazine, long since forgotten. Americans back then didn't mind Canadians coming down and sneakily adding "u" to their "colors" and changing their "centers" to "centres." Just so long as they shut up and kept drawing that water and hewing that wood, just like today.

Within a year, Roberts returned to free-lancing, if not to Canada, churning out books of poetry and prose by the hundreds — a veritable Layton or Berton. (See **Layton** and/or **Berton**, remaindered at a bookstore near you.)

In 1907, finding New York too small to contain his talent, not to mention the growing number of his own remaindered books, Roberts went off to England. He fought in France during the war, often on the battlefields as well as its bars, and rose to the rank of major, ever hopeful his career would be ranked major, as well.

In 1925, Roberts retired to Canada, where he met with great acclaim. Had he retired to Florida, like most Canadians, at least he would have been met with great weather. The country had grown sick of reading only Bliss Carman's poetry, and wondered what had ever happened to Charles "goddam" Roberts. It was still a very small country.

The now acclaimed author gave lectures and readings across Canada, was honoured by major awards and was even knighted in 1935, for having reached the age of seventy-five without having died. Hollywood does the same with its Oscars.

Roberts finally moved to Toronto, both still white, Anglo-Saxon and Protestant, and as smug as ever. He died in 1943, a revered man of letters. After all, had he not lived and worked in the States? Had he not gone to England? Now *that* was a man Canadians could respect.

Today Roberts is called the Father of Canadian Literature, although the Mother remains unknown. He was the inventor of the modern animal story, long before the animals took over federal politics. He helped capture the Maritimes, years before French fishermen did the same. And he recreated the outdoors in print, when most of his countrymen had more outdoors than they could handle in real life. But most of all, he had lived and worked in the United States and England.

FROM *THE BIRDS AND THE BEES* (1901)

LET ME TELL YOU 'bout the bird and the bees and the flowers and the trees, since the bird is on the wing; in fact, 'tis the wing that's on the bird.

It was not yet dawn, nor had the sun risen yet, to bring down its glorious sunlight upon a still dark mountain. And there, up in a tree — look up! — waaaaaaay up! — sat the nest, in which the young baby eaglets shook and flapped their little bitty wings under the far greater span of their handsome mother's. Wings.

Mrs. Eagle raised up her haughty head and peered about her, lifting her wings in a kind of shrug: Just another day for them and me in paradise. The little babies were peed off, for chill air had now ruffled their feathers. It was a lot warmer when they were still inside the egg, that was for sure. The male bird, not even married to the mother of his children, so to speak, if you get what I mean, nudge nudge wing wing, did not move, although he was fully awake. He looked up with his yellow eyes — it had been another late night with the owls — and watched Old Sol slowly spread his/her rays across the western — or is that eastern? (I usually focus on the animals) — sky.

The huge birds were starving, their bellies hungry for food, their beaks salivating, their innards longing to eat, my thesaurus is in the other room. For many days now, the mother and father eagle had searched in vain, but the fish were somehow gone, having all swum off to be described in my latest vignette, "Three Little Fishees in an Itty Bitty Lake," appearing in some American magazine or other in one of the next few issues. The many schools of herring and mackerel, both pickled and holy, had seemed to shun the nearby shores that famished spring, leaving the neighbourhood eagles and eaglets to scrounge for whatever they could find. In the area.

Suddenly the giant father eagle spotted a lamb — or did it spy a spotted lamb? — in the nearby, not-too-distant distance. Would it actually fly off and grab that baby lamb? Is that nice? Won't the mother lamb be really angry?

Oh, little lamb, who ate thee? Little lamb, who ate thee? It's just too horrible to describe, so I won't, except to say that the daddy eagle swooped down and caught the lamb in its talons, flying away with it to its hungry young, off in the nearby nest in the not faraway distance.

Nature sure can be brutal! The baby eaglets were happy; the little lamb didn't know what bit it; and the mother lamb, unable to read this exquisitely written story to tell it what happened to its baby, bleated "Hey, ewe!!! Ewe-hoooooo!" but to no avail. No one promised the lambs a rose garden, nor did the eagles get one either; they had lamb stew while the lamb's mother stewed. But at least the birds weren't hungry anymore.

Meanwhile, a group of bees swarmed in the tree below. . . .

SINCLAIR ROSS

(1908 –   )

SINCLAIR ROSS was born near Prince Albert, Saskatchewan, where his parents were homesteading. (Homesteading, of course, is different from prospecting, because in prospecting the person occasionally makes a living.) He grew up on farms on the prairies, and after his father died when he was only twelve (the boy, not the father), young Sinclair soon found himself in the money. This was because he worked as a bank clerk in various small towns in Saskatchewan, where many hundreds of dollars every year would flow into the banks' busy vaults.

Obviously a man who knew how to handle money well, Ross remained a banker all his life, with the exception of four years spent with the Canadian Army in England, where he tried to warm up. What with the lack of central heating in that country, however, it was useless.

As early as 1935, one of Sinclair Ross's fine short stories appeared in a British magazine, where it won third prize out of some eight thousand entries. For an American this would have been a mortification, but for Ross it was a thrill.

Most of his later stories appeared in *Queen's Quarterly*, which had no contest and paid practically nothing, but there was all that money in the bank, so he never had to worry.

In 1941, shortly before he headed off to fight the British during the Second World War, he published his first and most famous novel, *As for Me and My House*, which attracted almost no critical attention or sales for more than sixteen years. But, working in a bank, Ross knew how long these things could take. Try asking for a loan after writing the word "author" on the piece of paper they hand you, and you'll understand.

Sinclair Ross continued to work at the Royal Bank of Canada until his retirement in 1968, and if you were receiving book royalties like his, you would keep your job at the bank, too. Subsequently he spent several years in Greece and Spain, where he finally encountered decent weather. He returned to Canada in 1980 to live in Vancouver, a city where it hasn't stopped raining since 1892.

Although Ross has written several novels during his lengthy life, including *The Well* (1958), *Whir of Gold* (1970) and *Sawbones Memorial* (1974), as well as dozens of exceedingly impressive short stories (eighteen of which appeared in *The Lamp at Noon and Other Stories* in 1968), his fame rests primarily on his first novel about him and his house.

Throughout his work, it is clear that Ross, in spite of his decades of dipping his hand in the till and his impressive travels to Winnipeg, Montreal and finally Vancouver, never left the prairie farms at all, any more than **Mordecai Richler** ever left the Main in Montreal. This is a pattern in much of Canadian regional fiction: in the U.S., you can't go home again; in this country, it's impossible to get you to leave, at least in spirit.

THE PLOT OF *AS FOR ME AND MY HOUSE*

THE STORY OF THIS BOOK is in the form of Mrs. Bentley's diary, which seems okay, until you realize that Mrs. Bentley might not be telling the truth, which goes against everything that people believe about diaries. Mrs. Bentley is a small-town preacher's wife, who keeps this diary from the spring she and her husband (Philip Bentley) arrive in a new town named Horizon (which is a symbol and an irony, as any good eleventh-grade English teacher will prove to you), through the following spring, when the unhappy couple leave the tiny town for the tiny city, where they can be unhappy in a more congenial surroundings.

The United Church parish in Horizon is Philip Bentley's fourth ministry in a dozen years, suggesting either improprieties with the charity plate, a definite lack of tenure or a lack of excitement and satisfaction on the part of his various parishioners.

For Mrs. Bentley, who has so much time on her little hands she has to keep this diary that she might even be lying to and in, the new town is just one more cross to bear, which one would *think* would be quite an advantage to a minister's wife. You see, Philip Bentley longs to be an artist, and this is the Great Depression and the Canadian prairies, a one-two punch that would have knocked out George Chuvalo had he been fighting back then. Furthermore, Mrs. Bentley is childless — no thanks to Philip Bentley — even though with all that time on her hands in all those small prairie towns, you'd think she would have been in a family way by now. (Or else this sterility on the part of the Bentleys is one more symbol: ask that English teacher of yours to tell you.)

Impoverished, longing for children, longing for artistic fulfillment — and during the Great Depression, on the Canadian prairies yet — the Bentleys make a couple who can no way be confused with the Kramdens, much less the Ricardos. As one critic put it, "The Bentleys live a life of controlled despair," something rarely recommended by contemporary marriage counsellors. Their way of relating has reached the level of grunts, pointing, nods and shaking heads, possibly another reason that Mrs. Bentley hasn't conceived yet.

Then into this promising atmosphere lands Paul Kirby, a local schoolteacher, who becomes a frequent dinner guest; this is, after all, the Great Depression on the prairies, and even schoolteachers had to eat. (Ask your grade eleven teacher about that, as well.) He is a charming fellow, making the Bentleys chuckle for the first time in many years, as he plays word games with them, sort of like what Sinclair Ross is doing with this so far rather tedious novel.

Most important, Kirby introduces this dreary couple to a lad named Steve Kulanich, who (surprise) was abandoned by a loser of a father. He is also motherless, which impresses no one, since they remember when the czar was Nicholas. The Bentleys, anxious to have children without the mess of sex and the pain of childbirth, adopt the lad. It's an instant family, and both Philip and his wife are thrilled for the next two months, until some bigot or other in the parish notifies the local Catholic Church, which is horrified to hear that the poor child has been living with some lousy Protestants — one of whom is a United Church minister yet. They take the boy off to their orphanage, and you can just imagine what happens to him there. But we're never told, dammit.

Now that this one spark of happiness is out of the house, the spiritual malaise of the couple continues to grow —

about the only thing growing in that place except the silences between Philip and the missus. The wife now gets so ill physically that her good friend, Judith West, comes to nurse the woman back to health so she can return to her happy home situation once more. The reader can well understand why Mrs. Bentley is in no rush to get well.

Here's where it really gets exciting. It seems that Judith West — who is a member of the church choir, usually a hotbed of prairie voluptuousness — is attracted to Philip Bentley. (Let us recall that Mrs. Bentley was a fairly talented musician, who had longed for a career in the arts and settled for playing the organ in her husband's church, which could be a symbol, but I'm afraid to comment; this is a family book.)

One night Mrs. Bentley hears the laughter of Judith West from the shed near the house and suspects something. After all, laughter was not legal on the Canadian prairies during the entire period of the Great Depression, which lasted from 1929 until 1939, though many historians and other scholars suggest that it's still not over. The suffering wife is horrified, yet somehow not too surprised when Judith is discovered to be pregnant, and therefore must have been doing *something* in that shed — and back in the 1930s it sure wasn't artificial insemination. The young woman is driven from the town in disgrace and goes off to her family's home out in the country, which women used to do a lot in those days. But she refuses to tell anyone who her lover was, driving Mrs. Bentley and the reader to distraction, as well as back to Hawthorne's *Scarlet Letter*, another book with lots of laughs but from the United States and written some years earlier.

Now it's winter, which on the Canadian prairies lasts from only mid-September through June each year. The Bentleys continue to grow so far apart that Philip considers enlarging the house. Mrs. Bentley, overwhelmed with loneliness, adopts a stray dog named El Greco — this could also prove to be a symbol, and one with fleas, as well as meaning, since El Greco was a brooding Spanish painter who usually showed tortured souls on his canvases, even though he wasn't from the Canadian prairies — who accompanies her on her endless walks in the area.

Naturally, this not being a comic novel, El Greco becomes dinner for a pack of wolves one night. And Paul Kirby, fresh from the disastrous introduction of the Bentleys to that Catholic kid we mentioned earlier, falls deeply in love with Mrs. Bentley (even, I presume, calling her by her first name, which the reader never discovers). He is unaware, alas, that Mrs. Bentley is only using him to drive her husband bananas, as if being on the Canadian prairies during the Great Depression while serving as a United Church minister when you really want to be an artist weren't enough — not that bananas were even available in the country stores of the time.

The Bentleys finally figure out a way to end this endless despair, and it isn't by winning ten million dollars from a publishing house, either. The two of them decide to adopt Judith West's baby when it's finally born, take the hundreds of dollars that Mrs. Bentley has managed to scrimp and save, and buy a second-hand bookstore in a town nearby, where Philip will never have to create and deliver another tedious sermon again. Many readers maliciously assume there will be enough unsold books by Sinclair Ross to keep Bentley busy for years.

The Bentleys now tell Judith West about their big plans, which is good of them; most women giving up their babies for adoption enjoy knowing they're doing it. She reacts with a desperation characteristic of mortified, shamed women on the Canadian prairies during the 1930s, when they were a dime a dozen. The baby is born a month prematurely — would that the book ended prematurely — and West dies the day after the delivery, which certainly eliminates further complications, just in case she had planned to reveal who the father was, which is what happened in the Hawthorne book we mentioned earlier.

The novel ends with the Bentleys taking the baby with them as they prepare to leave the charming, picturesque town of Horizon for a new town beyond the horizon. It's just one big happy Canadian family now: a former minister who wanted to be an artist, who's now about to open a used bookstore and who once accused his wife of adultery; a barren, depressed woman who longed to be a musician and who still suspects her husband of adultery; a new baby who may or may not be the product of the husband's adultery; and another small town in the Canadian prairies during the Great Depression. Any resemblance to *Lady Oracle*, *Turvey* or *Sunshine Sketches* is purely coincidental.

GABRIELLE ROY

(1909 – 1983)

ROY was a French-Canadian author who actually came from Manitoba, which really shouldn't be surprising, since there are politicians in Ottawa who come from the Maritimes who can't even speak English. Born in St. Boniface at a time when Quebeckers still cared about whether French people existed outside their province, she was educated there, taught in smaller communities in Manitoba, studied theatre in Europe and eventually moved to Quebec to become a writer. (Interestingly, many Canadians, such as **Mordecai Richler**, had to *leave* Quebec to become writers. This could have something to do with the two solitudes you've heard about; see **MacLennan, Hugh**, but avoid the movie.)

Over nearly four decades, Roy produced a number of most interesting books, such as *Where Nests the Water Hen* (1951); *The Cashier* (1955); *Street of Riches* (1957); *The Road Past Altamont* (1966); and several other works, most of them filled with loneliness, despair and women who have a baby every few months like clockwork. (The latter thoroughly confused the Québécois, who had stopped having babies in the early 1960s, to the horror of provincial politicians; presumably the "*Je me souviens*" on their licence plates had been used by the public to remind them to use birth control.)

Gabrielle Roy's greatest success was her widely praised and internationally best-selling first novel, *Bonheur d'occasion*, in 1945, translated into English as *The Tin Flute*. It is a moving portrayal of a slum family in Montreal, the Lacasses, who have suffered through the Great Depression, but luckily in only one official language. Azarius, the father, is a carpenter who has not held down a steady job for years, which already explains why the book became a Literary Guild choice in New York and captured the revered Prix Femina in Paris: the entire world wanted to read about impoverished French-Canadian families where the father had not worked for years. His wife, Rose-Anna, a slave to the kitchen, the laundry and her four dozen children is determined and pathetic; the only question mark in her daily existence is whether she'll ever see a period. No, she'd probably go into a comma first.

Every year we encounter poor, preggers Rose-Anna, forever walking the streets of Montreal (no, not that; this novel was written in the forties), looking for another tiny, filthy house in which to move her children, who now number some fifty-seven. She eventually finds a house, which has to be painted before it can be legally condemned. Then, when she moves the growing family into another place, it is immediately torn down so that the city government can put up a slum. Lacking terribly in both clothes and food, the children, who now number close to one hundred, grow up cold, hungry, undereducated and not the type to join the Literary Guild Book Club. The happy news is that one of the Lacasse children (yes, there are some 130 at this point in the novel), Florentine, helps to support the family with the huge sums she is taking in while working as a waitress, and meets an inevitably fertile young factory worker, Jean Lévesque (yes, even in the slums of Montreal, everyone loves to social climb), who gets her in a family way, which comes as no surprise. He understandably abandons her (*These men*! See **Atwood, Margaret**), so she ends up marrying a young soldier, Emmanuel, who doesn't know that he's getting slightly used merchandise, but what a charming surprise awaits him when he receives her first letter while overseas.

Things really come together for Flo's Lacasse family by the end of the book. One brother dies of leukemia; another brother goes off to war; her father goes off to war, as well (providing him with his first work, aside from impregnating his wife, in a number of years); and a sister decides to become a nun, seemingly the only way to prevent these people from getting pregnant. The Yankees and French had good cause to love this book. These were the French Canadians they had learned to treasure in **Louis Hémon**'s *Maria Chapdelaine*. And the Anglos loved it, as well, since the novel made it look as though the French Canadians were actually eager to fight during the Second World War. So everybody was happy, especially Rose-Anna Lacasse, who, with her husband going off to fight in Europe, would be able to give her uterus a much needed rest.

JANE RULE

(1931 –)

THE fine writer who has worked hard and with great literary skill to change the image of Galiano Island, B.C., to that of the Isle of Lesbos.

GEORGE RYGA

(1932 – 1987)

AS one of Canada's most famous Ukrainian authors, Ryga naturally became the voice of the Canadian Indian. (This was years before it was racist for non-Indians to write about the Indian experience; see **Kinsella, W. P.**) After seven years in a one-room schoolhouse in Deep Creek, Alberta, where he was never taught that the Holocaust hadn't happened, since it *hadn't* happened yet, he did a number of odd jobs, ranging from construction, to working on a farm, to the depths of human degradation — working as a radio producer in Edmonton.

Ryga's greatest success was *The Ecstasy of Rita Joe*, in 1967, about a Canadian Indian who does about as well in big-city Canada as Ryga's family would have done in Stalin's Ukraine. Although he went on to write many, many more plays, novels, short stories and poetry, he was never again as successful with any work (see **Herbert, John**). His plays have been extremely popular across both Western and Eastern Europe, however, on both radio and stage, winning awards and huge audiences, since both Western and Eastern Europeans love to see Canadians brutalize their native population, just as Canadians have always enjoyed looking at the treatment of blacks in the U.S. and South Africa and feeling superior.

In Ryga's work, the Indians are all put-upon and mistreated; the whites are all malevolent or useless. This is known in theatrical terms as realism.

FROM *THE ECSTASY OF RITA JOE*

MAGISTRATE (*Condescending*)
Well, you stupid drunken Indian broad, do you want a crooked, evil, corrupt white lawyer or not?

RITA JOE
What for? I have all the crooked, evil, corrupt social workers I need back on the reservation.

MAGISTRATE
I can't say I blame you. If you knew the crooked, evil, corrupt white lawyers I'm forced to listen to, every single day . . .

RITA JOE (*With a sad sigh*)
It's worse for me, your Dishonour! Every native *I* know is pure of heart, decent, kindly, sweet and honest. It's as tedious as a visit to Ottawa.

MAGISTRATE
Enough philosophizing, Rita Joe! The charge

against you this morning is prostitution, which gives me a charge just to mention it. Why did you not return to your people as you promised you would?

RITA JOE (*Demure*)
Oh, I tried, your Dishonour. I did try. But every bus driver tried to fondle me, and every train conductor tried to grab me, and every —

MAGISTRATE (*Cruel and unfeeling*)
It wouldn't happen if you weren't so darned cute, Rita Joe. And your dresses are too short, which only drives evil, corrupt, vulgar white men crazy. So it's all your fault, when you come to think of it. You really should improve your makeup, try to get rid of that irritatingly non-Canadian accent.

RITA JOE
You're cruel and heartless and unfeeling and racist!

MAGISTRATE (*Sweet, but still unfeeling*)
But I have to be, Rita Joe. I'm a white judge, in a system that was specifically set up to deny the natives their rights. You really should have figured all this out by now. I'm afraid that I'm going to have to . . .

RITA JOE (*Horrified*)
Send me to jail?

Enter JAIMIE PAUL, *her boyfriend*

JAIMIE PAUL (*Rushing in*)
Worse, Rita Joe. He's going to call in the singer!

RITA JOE (*Falling to her knees; begging*)
No! No! Not the singer! Not that simpy, liberal, white singer! I can't take her! I don't understand how the white audience can take her, either!

Enter the SINGER

SINGER (*Simpy, liberal*)
Oh, their hearts soar like an eagle
While they're treated as badly as a beagle.
Who offers these natives a bagel
Just 'cause they've never studied Hegel?

RITA JOE (*Weeping for mercy*)
Take her away! Oh, please, dear God. Take her away!!

SINGER (*Ignoring her pleas; simpy*)
Can't you see the train comin' down the track?
Bein' Indian is almost as rough as bein' black.
There ain't no justice in this crummy land —
But at least in Romania and Albania, things are grand. . . .

RITA JOE (*Still begging for mercy*)
Look, your Dishonour, I realize that you're white, and therefore cruel, unfair, dishonest and generally meanspirited, but couldn't you get that singer out of here?

MAGISTRATE (*Grinning maliciously*)

I'm afraid there's nothing more I can do, Rita Joe. She's going to share your cell with you.

RITA JOE (*Crushed into submission*)
Why? Why me? And why her? I was a prostitute. But she's white and liberal — so what did she do to be sent to jail?

JAIMIE PAUL (*Crushed by a train into submission*)
Are you kiddin', Rita Joe? Just listen to those lyrics! She'll probably get twenty years for Commie sympathizing.

SINGER (*Oblivious, as always*)
This ain't no world for native folk,
The whites just want them all to croak. . . .

RITA JOE (*Giving in*)
Please! Lock me up! Throw away the key! And find out what key that honky is singing in, if you can. . . .

RICH SALUTIN

(1942 –)

To paraphrase a classic line, Salutin's many leftist plays and essays are all far more gauche than they are sinister.

CHARLES SANGSTER

(1822 – 1893)

Born at the naval yard in Kingston, Ontario, the famous Canadian poet would contemplate his navel until the day of his death. His grandfather had been a United Empire Loyalist and his father had joined the British Navy: clearly, the only route open to young Charles was to pen unreadable poetry.

Sangster had a poor education, not unlike the majority of Canadian children today, more than 150 years later, except his excuse was that he had to drop out of school at the age of fifteen to support his mother. Well, that's the excuse he *gave*. He worked in the naval yard, edited a newspaper and eventually became a bookkeeper and proofreader at the Kingston *Whig* for nearly a dozen years, long before it became standard.

By 1864, Sangster was a reporter on the staff of the Kingston *Daily News*, missing the really big scoop of that decade: the American Civil War. But that's what it's like to live in Canada: the action always seems to be someplace else.

Then, when the Civil Service of the new Dominion of Canada was created in Ottawa, students of his poetry in the national capital just *knew* that Sangster had what it took to make a really great civil servant. He accepted a position in the newly formed Post Office — he was forty-six, so it was time for a midlife crisis, if not a career change — where he worked (a euphemism; this was the Post Office, please recall) for many years. He eventually died in Kingston, Ontario, presumably of boredom.

Sangster had been publishing his poems in the Kingston newspapers and in small Canadian magazines for sums about the same as they pay today. His two books were well received in Canada, which can be readily explained: there was no TV, no video, no radio; there just wasn't anything else to *do*. In 1864, in the first major anthology of Canadian literature in this country, *Selections from Canadian Poets*, Sangster was proclaimed the great white hope of Canada.

And white he was.

DUNCAN CAMPBELL SCOTT

(1862 – 1947)

THE son of yet another minister, in this case Methodist, Duncan Campbell Scott was one more holier-than-thou Canadian writer. All through his childhood, Scott's family moved from one small community to another, across eastern Ontario and western Quebec, presumably one step ahead of the cops. In the latter province during that time, knowledge of French was not yet considered an asset.

By the time Scott was fifteen, the family had finally settled in Stanstead, where the unrebellious teenager attended the then new Wesleyan College. He had hoped to become a doctor, but the family lacked the money and scholarships were unavailable for people of Scott's ethnic background, who numbered only about ninety-seven percent of the population.

While still in his teens, Scott joined the Department of Indian Affairs in Ottawa as a copy clerk, where there were few Indians but heap big'um bureaucracy. It was a perfect meeting of minds: the son of a minister who didn't know what he was doing and a ministry that had no idea what it was doing.

Scott took to his new job like a Scot to Canada, and by the age of fifty, he was in the highest position one could attain at the Department of Indian Affairs without smoking a questionable peace pipe. The civil servant was obsessed with Canada's native people — those that were still alive — and he began to write about them with warmth, intimate knowledge and, sadly, great copiousness.

Admirably, Scott had shown no interest in poetry until he was in his mid-twenties, when he met Archibald Lampman, who influenced him greatly, in spite of his silly given name. Within a few years, Lampman joined Scott — along with Wilfred Campbell — and they all began to write a weekly column in the Toronto *Globe*, "At the Mermaid Inn." (This was many years before the paper became "Canada's National Newspaper" and, eventually, "Canada's National Business Paper.") The column's huge popularity is suggested by the year and a half for which it ran.

After Lampman died at an early age, Scott served as his friend's literary executor, although he had nothing whatsoever to do with the other poet's execution. Indeed, he worked for years to keep his dear friend's work and name in the spotlight by refusing to let sleepy doggerel lie.

In 1894, Scott served as a piano accompanist at an Ottawa concert for a violinist from Boston. This led to their marriage (it was a woman), which marked the important beginning of a warm relationship between Boston and Canada. In fact, some eighty-four percent of all Maritimers have chosen to live in the Boston area today.

Scott's first collection of poems came out in 1893, with several copies purchased by the public by 1897 or so. It was entitled *The Magic House and Other Poems*, and was followed a few short years later by a collection of short stories and articles from various magazines, *In the Village of Viger*. The villagers of Viger loved it.

Then came several other books of poems, followed by more collections of poetry and prose. Scott was a man who did not know when to stop, even if his readers quickly did.

In 1932, Scott finally retired from the Civil Service, which was pretty retiring, anyway. (Clearly he hadn't been doing much on the job, since he found the time to put out such an endless profusion of books.) He then travelled around the world with his new wife — his first wife had died; this is Canada, remember — and continued to write poems until he was well into his eighties. See what comes from having too much time on your hands?

When Duncan Campbell Scott no longer published any more books after the summer of 1947, everyone figured he had died, and they were correct in the assumption. Doctoral students across the country mourned.

At the Cedars
(1893)

You had these girls — Pierre!
One was Céline —
What a scene — Pierre!
So be aware!

The logs were clogged
At that bog at the cedars,
The water was dammed
And all was crammed
With logs that bammed
(No pigs were hammed)
They sure were clammed and slammed!

We worked for days, we
Were not too lazy
We had logs to clear
They were too near
So we drank beer
But lacked all cheer
For we had fear
Of what was near.
(These rhymes! Oh, dear!)

The logs gave 'way!
Oh, unhappy day!
My friend, dear Jean

He jumped upon
The logs — soon gone!
Insurance, none,
The son of a gun.

Poor Jean was crushed
His brains were smushed
While all were hushed
No more he lushed!
His guts squashed and gushed.

Ah, yes, Pierre!
Some girls were there.
They saw Jean drown,
His pants fell down.
Your poor Céline!
Her love was green,
To her canoe
She flew
And to her Jean
She was soon drawn.

Pierre!
Mon frère!
Quel dommage!
Have some *fromage*?

F. R. SCOTT

(1899 – 1985)

LAW professor and dean, social critic, cofounder of the *McGill Fortnightly Review*, publisher of **A. M. Klein** and **P. K. Page**, involved with the founding of the *Tamarack Review*, hero to two generations of Canadian poets and surely the writer of the funniest poetry in Canada since the Confederation poets wrote funny poetry unintentionally.

ROBERT W. SERVICE

(1874 – 1958)

BORN in Preston, England and raised in Scotland, Robert William Service already had the two most important attributes for success in late-nineteenth-century Canada: he was born in England and he was raised in Scotland. Then he added a third guarantee: he worked for a bank in Scotland for seven years before moving to the only country on earth that has more banks than lawyers — Canada.

It was wanderlust that brought Service to the young colony; real lust was for the Mediterranean types, who wouldn't be able to get in for another half century. He worked on a farm in the backwoods of British Columbia, and began to wander up and down the west coast of the continent, from Mexico up to Vancouver Island, in search of an honest man. He eventually gave up and returned to the ranch on Vancouver Island.

Then it was back to banking, this time with the Bank of Commerce in Victoria in 1903. Suddenly he was transferred to Whitehorse, Yukon, in 1904, and eventually to Dawson, which would inspire his best-known verse. (Verse, as opposed to poetry.) Had he been transferred to a bank in Mexico, Sam McGee might have been cremated in a burrito.

By 1909, Service's verse had become popular right across the continent, from *Songs of a Sourdough* (1907) to

The Spell of the Yukon (1907) to *Ballads of a Cheechako* (1909) to *Rhymes of a Rolling Stone* (1912), many years before rock and roll ever made the scene.

Service turned out verse like sausages — indeed, you wouldn't want to know what went into either — as well as popular fiction, with such Canadian themes as *The Pretender: a Story of the Latin Quarter* (1914) and *The Roughneck: a Tale of Tahiti* (1923).

But Canada's North was not sufficient to contain such a man. He soon headed off to France, where he bought homes (with Canadian dollars) in Paris, Brittany and on the Riviera, even picking up a French wife along the way. He also travelled to the Balkans, Hollywood, Tahiti and even Russia, where the weather was still better than it was back in the Yukon. Yet, a true Canadian to the end, he spent World War II in Hollywood, and died in France in 1958. Many of his books of verse are still in print, more than three decades after his death, enraging serious Canadian poets from coast to coast.

From *The Shooting of Canadian McFlicks*

A bunch of the boys — both lawyers and docs —
were hoping their money to hide;
The bastards at Revenue Canada were hot to
prove they'd lied;
Back of the room, in a fit o' gloom, sat Dangerous
Canadian McFlicks,
Anxious to take their cash and run, and leave them
as broke as hicks.

When out of the night, like a MURB in flight,
came the chance to invest in some show,

And the suckers all bit — they were flattered by
it — as their savings they quickly did blow.
"You can write it off!" cried McFlicks (with a
cough), "and you'll get all your names up in
lights!"
So Canadian McFlicks took their money real quick,
and then vanished into the night.

So from *Circle of Two* and *Bethune* (Commie true!)
the films began to be made,
Although few saw the light, some suckers took
flight, as their money all started to fade.
They thought they'd make riches, those
sonsofobitches, and believed they'd be up on
a screen.
But Canadian McFlicks burst in flames like sticks,
And never again were they seen.
(Except on pay TV — with its great Can-Con
pleas —
And some ladies have been known to sue.)

Ernest Thompson Seton

(1860 – 1946)

For the birds.

Josef Skvorecky

(1924 –)

Brilliant emigré, brilliant immigrant, brilliant novelist, whose coming to Canada helped prevent him from becoming just one more cancelled Czech (see **Newman, Peter C.**). Since 1971, Skvorecky and his wife have been the single most important publishers of dissident literature in his native tongue. He has sold his writings to eager followers all over the world, giving a whole new Canadian meaning to the expression "the Czech is in the mail."

RAYMOND SOUSTER

(1921 –)

THE man who chose to be to Toronto what Joyce was to Dublin, Dickens was to London and Tom Wolfe is to New York: its singer, its artist, its painter, its glorifier, its capturer-in-print. Of course, in the case of Souster, he had all the luck, since he worked for the Canadian Imperial Bank of Commerce for more than four decades and thus was in an ideal position to capture the city's $oul.

CATHARINE PARR TRAILL

(1802 – 1899)

CATHARINE Parr Traill had one great advantage shared by many early writers of Canada: she was born in England. Furthermore, her maiden name was Strickland, which gave her an almost immediate recognition factor at the time: one sister, Agnes, was to gain fame in England as a writer of historical works; another sister, Susanna, became moody and a famous author in her own right. How right she was, you were able to judge a few more pages back.

Indeed, it was with her sister **Susanna Moodie**, as well

as her brother-in-law, that Catharine Parr Strickland trailled behind her husband to a new home and native land.

The year was 1832, which was a great time to buy land cheap in downtown Toronto. Alas, the family chose to settle near Rice Lake, in eastern Ontario, where house prices have remained relatively stable ever since. It was here that Traill would pen *The Backwoods of Canada*, a title that would not guarantee any wild bidding over movie rights and that was published in England, because no Canadian publisher was interested. Or even existed. **Mavis Gallant** later moved to France for similar reasons.

The subtitle of *Backwoods* is important to note, and it just could be on the exam: "Being Letters from the Wife of an Emigrant Officer, Illustrative of the Domestic Economy of British America." One can readily understand why Hollywood has yet to option her work.

Traill's book was published a full dozen years before her sister, Susanna Moodie, hit the best-seller lists, but this came as no shock to the latter (younger by one year); their mother had always loved Catharine better, anyway, and both girls knew it. (Grown women were called girls back then.)

Long extracts from *Backwoods* were published in the Canadian magazines of the time, although even in the nineteenth century, Canadians preferred American entertainment. Traill was publishing even into her nineties, which would have made her the dean, or deaness, of Canadian literature of the time, had there been any Canadian literature of the time. Legend has it that the people from the funeral home had to pry the pen out of her hands in order to stop Mrs. Traill from doing any posthumous writing. Indeed, few authors in this country's history took their work so seriously. Would that their readers felt the same way.

MICHEL TREMBLAY

(1942 –)

THE Great Poet of Montreal, Michel Tremblay was born with printing ink in his veins. Not that he was naturally talented as a writer, but because both his father and his brother were Linotype operators. Although Michel studied toward the same goal, he won a Radio-Canada prize with his very first play, when he was still in his teens, and realized it would be even more fun if someone else laid the type for him.

Tremblay's big breakthrough was *Les Belles-sœurs*, first produced in 1968. It was a wild success and heralded the beginning of a fruitful and fruity career of expressing the true nature of Québécois society: frustrated women, alienated men, women frustrated by alienated men, men alienated from frustrated women, an overwhelming church, powerless women, doomed men, powerless men, doomed women and powerless and doomed homosexual men. Fortunately there is transvestism and incest, along with suicide and drunkenness, to take the edge off the occasional "downer themes" (to use **Northrop Frye**'s literary term).

His plays are crucially important to Canada because they are written primarily in *joual*, the true language of the French Canadian, sort of like Yiddish for **Richler**'s Jews and Inarticulateness for most other writers' Protestants.

Today Tremblay is, *sans doute*, the most widely read and performed Québécois playwright in the world, who has done for the East End of Montreal what **Margaret Laurence** did for Manitoba, **George Ryga** did for Indians and the Turks did for Armenians.

His plays, thankfully, are filled with good humour and much laughter, along with self-hatred, masochism, sadism, bitterness and rage, as well as those two Québécois favourites, powerlessness and frustration. Not to mention homosexuality, incest, family violence and lots of other things to temper the laughter a bit. In *Les Belles-sœurs*, fifteen women help a good friend paste trading stamps into hundreds of books, then steal the books from her. In *A toi pour toujours, ta Marie-Lou* (1973), two daughters of wretched parents, who fortunately died before the play begins, choose between being wretched and unhappy like their parents and singing country-and-western songs in a sleazy nightclub, which is known *en français* as "*le choix de Hobson.*"

In *Saint Carmen de la Main* (1976), our country-and-western singer returns to the Main, where she hangs around with whores and cross-dressers, a subtle reference to the Quebec Liberal Party. Then there's *Hosanna* (1973), in which a man spends the entire play getting dressed up like Elizabeth Taylor, when the dream of the vast majority of men, both in the province of Quebec and outside *la belle province*, has always been to get Elizabeth Taylor *un*dressed. Sadly, the play was produced twice in New York City and flopped both times, perhaps because that city has had more than enough men dressing up like Elizabeth Taylor.

Men have always been weak, disgusting and brutal in most Canadian literature, so this is nothing new. But Michel Tremblay has brought a new reality to this country's theatre that cannot be denied or ignored: men aren't always even men.

FROM *LES BELLES-SŒURS*

GERMAINE
Allo? Lisette? Here they are! Ten million stamps! Wait till you see da catalogue for dis year! I'll be able to buy an oppressive church, or an impotent man, or a corrupt politician, or an unhappy, maladjusted child! I'm rich! I'm rich! Hey, Thérèse! Is that your mother-in-law you've come in with?

THERESE (*Slugging the old woman across the head*)
She's fine now. I learned dat from my husband. Just a good wallop across the head, and she acts real good.

DES-NEIGES (*Coming in to paste stamps*)
Did you hear da one about the priest and nun who couldn't decide who would do da raising of der kids?

LISETTE (*Overhearing; licking stamps*)
Shame on you, Des-Neiges! You ought to have your mouth washed out with Pepsi!! It is always da *man* who should be responsible for da raising of da children!!

DES-NEIGES (*Licking, then stealing stamps*)
Oh, but *I* need a man, bad!!

LINDA (*Stealing stamps she licked*)
Bad men? They're a dime a dozen. But a man who will hit you where it doesn't show too much? *They* are very rare indeed!

YVETTE (*Swallowing stamps with Pepsi-Cola*)
I hear your daughter is pregnant again, Marie-Ange!

MARIE-ANGE (*Soaking stamps in pea soup*)
C'est vrai, c'est vrai, Yvette. But we don't believe in birth control, as you know. Besides, she's almost ten, so it's about time dat she settles down, you know?

LISE (*Chewing on stamps*)
Linda, I have to tell someone! I'm going to have a baby!

LINDA (*Cooking stamps with frogs' legs*)
But that's horrible!

LISE (*Hiding stamps in bassinet*)
Not really. It's by my own brudder, so at least we kept *le scandale* in da family.

LINDA (*Crossing herself with stamps*)
Thank God for that! But you know, Morgenthaler *is* legal in Quebec, you know.

LISE (*Shocked, as she stuffs stamps into bra*)
That would be a mortal sin!!

PIERRETTE (*Enraged; tossing stamps out window*)

Do you know what sort of bastard I married? He beat me up, then used me like a pimp in his night club, and now I feel like I'm only fit to jump off a bridge. God, why couldn't I have fallen in love with a homosexual?

ROSE (*English-kissing her stamps*)
No such luck. They're all writing plays and don't have any time for intelligent, cultured women like us. . . .

MIRIAM WADDINGTON

(1917 –   )

AN often terrific poet, especially writing about the Canadian people, love and loss (the last two often a redundancy). Her specifically ethnic work is also fine, but many Canadians find that it's all Yiddish to them.

GEORGE F. WALKER

(1947 –   )

THE incredibly successful Canadian playwright was born in Toronto and raised in its east end. In 1970, while driving a cab, he saw a notice on a lamppost, requesting scripts for a newly founded theatre. In response, Walker wrote his first play (*Prince of Naples*, 1972), and followed it by well over a dozen more, including *Beyond Mozambique* (1974), *Zastrozzi* (1977), *Filthy Rich* (1979), *Criminals in Love* (1984), *Nothing Sacred* (1988) and *Love and Anger* (1989), many of which have been performed around the world. It makes one wonder what would have happened if the notice on the lamppost had been for a bank robber. Would Walker have become a master of crime?

Although most of Walker's plays have been applauded around the world, his greatest single success was undoubtedly *Nothing Sacred*, based on a major novel by Turgenev. The thought that one's most successful work is essentially an adaptation has frightened many a writer, and the jury is still out about whether Walker can do as well on his own. Lord knows, with Toronto tending to be his subject matter in most plays, he could have his work cut out for him.

SHEILA WATSON

(1909 –)

MORE than any other Canadian writer, Sheila Watson had the perfect background for writing literature: as a child, she lived on the grounds of a mental hospital in New Westminster, British Columbia, where her father worked as superintendent. True, she spent much of her youth in convent schools, which can be similarly inspiring, but those years in the asylum wing surely gave her all the ideas she would need — not to mention the necessary background — to teach successfully in elementary-school classrooms in Dog Creek, Langley Prairie, Duncan and Mission City, B.C.

It was during the few years she lived in Calgary that she wrote her most celebrated novel, *The Double Hook* (1959), a true prose poem, in which Ara is sterile, Greta commits suicide, Mrs. Potter is murdered and Christian and pagan symbolism blur as much as at a Social Credit town-hall meeting. The novel became almost a cult book among Canadian university students, who are usually eager to join any cult they can find. The novel's author became *persona non grata* to the people of Dog Creek, B.C., who didn't appreciate her depiction of their town any more than the Montreal Jewish community loved the writings of **Mordecai Richler** — who, many survivors of St. Urbain Street would admit, *also* grew up on the grounds of an insane asylum.

RUDY WIEBE

(1934 –)

THE originator of the concept "a community of communities" even before Prime Minister Joe Clark came up with the line, Rudy Wiebe is the ultimate regional writer, since he is hooked up through fax machines with regional movements in Latin America and the United States.

Born to Russian Mennonite parents near Fairholme, Saskatchewan, Wiebe attended a Mennonite high school in Coaldale, Alberta many years before being ethnic in Canada was considered "in." After briefly studying in West Germany, where he would watch all the Canadian-built Starfighters go down in flames every few days, he earned a Master of Arts in creative writing at the University of Alberta in 1960. He then taught at the Mennonite Brethren Bible College, and even edited the *Mennonite Brethren Herald*, not unlike Hemingway's and **Callaghan**'s work at the *Toronto Star*, a larger socialist paper to the east. He also taught English at the University of Alberta in Edmonton for many years, even though he wasn't Ukrainian.

In the best tradition of Canadian writing, Wiebe has chosen to write about what he knows best. Two of his early novels, *Peace Shall Destroy Many* (1962) and *The Blue*

Mountains of China (1970) deal with, as their titles suggest, the Mennonite experience in North America, while other books, such as *The Temptation of Big Bear* (1973) and *The Scorched-Wood People* (1977), focus on the Indians and Métis of Canada's Northwest and their rebellion against their oppressors, both of which happened quite a bit before Wiebe's time.

What's most important to Wiebe is that he is a westerner and a Mennonite (something that makes him eligible for more than $145,000 every single year in multicultural grants). He is obsessed with man's attempts to live a decent, ethical life in a world that is violent, grotesque and vile (you know, like British Columbia provincial politics). And in a number of novels, Wiebe is concerned with the question of how to live a Christian life in a world that doesn't seem to care — something that never seemed to bother **Richler, Layton, A. M. Klein** and **Leonard Cohen** at all.

Like **George Ryga**, who was interested in the Canadian Indian, Wiebe has also turned to our native people as subject matter, even though it's racist for him to do so. Still, with a writing as flowing as a prairie dog in a microwave, and with an obvious inability to pay his own syntax, Wiebe continues to challenge his many fans, most of whom wait anxiously for his novels and short stories to be translated into English.

ETHEL WILSON

(1888 – 1980)

BORN in South Africa before it was a crime to have been, to a missionary father and a mother who both died on her at an early age, Ethel Wilson came to Canada in 1898 and lived in Vancouver with her grandmother. In moving to Canada's West Coast after having been born elsewhere, Wilson parallels **Malcolm Lowry**, except that she was not an alcoholic, she didn't wander across Mexico and she wasn't a man — already three strikes against her.

Wilson did not begin publishing her impressive short stories and novels until she was nearly fifty — something we would have heartily recommended to several of the writers profiled in this book — and for some fifteen years after World War II, she published some half-dozen novels and many short stories. Her words were admired in the United States and England as well as back home in Canada, which means that several are still read in Canadian literature courses today in numerous universities. Her best known novels are *Hetty Dorval* (1947) and *Swamp Angel* (1954). With these she managed to put the British Columbian interior on the map, something that Rand McNally had failed to do for a number of years. In depicting the evils of gossip, the jealousy of women and the revered tradition of men deserting their wives, Wilson inspired such future Canadian writers as **Margaret Laurence** and **Alice Munro**.

All critics agree that to read the solid fiction of Ethel Wilson is to truly understand how middle-class people talked, lived and loved in British Columbia in the 1940s, long before W.A.C. Bennett and his son came in to destroy the middle class forever.

ADELE WISEMAN

(1928 –)

IN two major novels, as well as several lesser works, Winnipeg-born Adele Wiseman has attempted to recreate the powerful immigrant experience of Jews coming to Canada — something that wasn't a lot of fun, if we can judge by *The Sacrifice* (1956) and *The Crackpot* (1974). In the former novel, which won the Governor General's Award, even though it was a great book, we encounter Abraham, his son Isaac and his grandson Moses, which would confuse even Northrop Frye, who prides himself on knowing his Bible backward and forward. Actually, it's his Hebrew that Frye knows backward and forward, and his Bible, forward and backward.

Anyway, Abraham becomes a butcher, which in Winnipeg was once a prestigious occupation, his son Isaac dies in a synagogue fire and Abraham ends up slitting the throat of a prostitute, which is about as far from proper butcher protocol as a person can get. He goes mad and is committed to a mental hospital, which thankfully is warmer than his old butcher shop in downtown Winnipeg. In spite of the violence of the novel, it actually displays a warmth, affection and understanding for the author's coreligionists, unlike the novels of some other Canadian writers we can think of (*don't* see **Richler, Mordecai**).

GEORGE WOODCOCK

(1912 –   )

GEORGE Woodcock was born in Winnipeg but taken to England by his parents as a child — a complete reversal of what British children experienced a decade later during World War II. There Woodcock was forced to spend his formative years with George Orwell, E. M. Forster and other non-Canadians writing at that time, before finally returning to his native land in 1949. Over the next four decades he edited *Canadian Literature* magazine, published countless books about

India, Asia, Mexico and South America, wrote and published books about British Columbia and Canada, created studies on major political movements, penned many definitive biographies and profiles of important Canadians, from Gabriel Dumont to **Malcolm Lowry**, as well as less famous non-Canadians such as Aldous Huxley, Oscar Wilde and others, dashed off several volumes of autobiography and . . .

Let's put it this way. If any student reading this book is asked, "Who wrote ——— " and the work is by a Canadian, if the answer isn't **Pierre Berton**, it's more than likely George Woodcock.